AF269207

What I Know About the Human Race

A Collection of Writing

Christian Fennell

Montreal Publishing Company

ISBN: 978-1-998353-00-2

What I Know About the Human Race/Christian Fennell—1st Edition.
June/2024

Any references to historical events, real people, or real places are used fictitiously. Names, characters, and places are products of the author's imagination.

Cover: Nelligan Design
Montreal Publishing Company
montrealpublishing.com

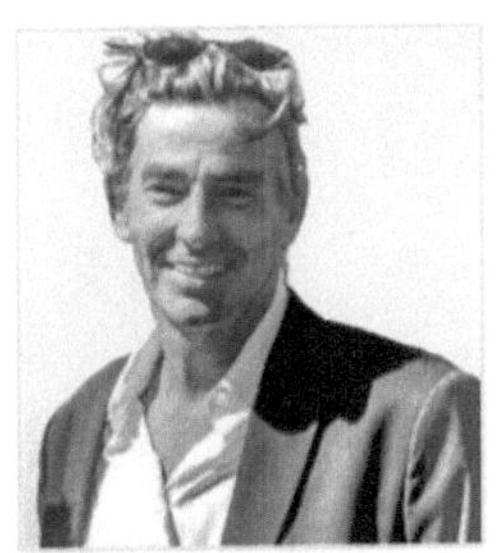

Christian Fennell is the author of the critically acclaimed collection of short stories, Torrents of Our Time, and the novels, The Fiddler in the Night, and LOVE, GUNS & GOD in America. He was a columnist and the Fiction Editor at The Prague Revue, and is currently the Editor-in-chief of The Nelligan Review. Christian resides in North Hatley, QC.

Other Books by Christian Fennell

Torrents of Our Time
The Fiddler in the Night
LOVE, GUNS & GOD in America

Torrents of Our Time:

Whatever expectations one might have of a book of dark, realist short stories set in rural America, this collection defies them, and instead weaves an elegant song of sadness, dark humour, and strangeness."- *Neon Books UK*

"Many of Fennell's stories, which employ different narrative techniques, create effective tension and suspense." - *Kirkus Reviews*

"This book is simply Douglas Adams but written for small-town America. This is a Hitchhiker's Guide to small-town America." - *Book Heaven*

"Christian Fennell writes stories to savour. Sharp, salty and sly, they come at you sideways with a shot of poignancy when you least expect it - and a twist of humour when you most need it." - Katy Darby, Director, *Liars' League London*

The Fiddler in the Night:

"In essence, the author has created a work of art in word form." - *The US Review of Books*

"Fennell's haunting and poetic prose takes readers through the Godforsaken terrain of rural America on a wild ride to its stunning and heartbreaking conclusion."
- *San Francisco Book Review*

"Haunting and ethereal, Fennell's stand-alone The Fiddler in the Night is a masterpiece of reflection that is at once gritty, disturbing, and hard to put down."
- *Midwest Book Review*

"This dark coming-of-age story will impress readers with its distinctive writing and intense, at times violent, story."
- *Booklife Reviews*

LOVE, GUNS & GOD in America:

"Christian Fennell's novel presents a vivid, soul-searching account of life and death in America. Passionate observations of life in different strata of the American psyche drive a story that is a raw inspection of the violence and confrontations of both a nation and the individual. Ultimately, LOVE, GUNS & GOD in America is a study in reality, adversity, shifting perspectives, and the courage to change." - *Midwest Book Review*

I am a second born.

A witness.

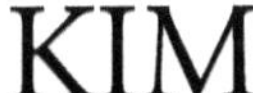

“He thought that God’s goodness appeared in strange places. Dont close your eyes.”

- Cormac McCarty

What I Know About the Human Race

A Collection of Writing

Christian Fennell

Montreal Publishing Company

TABLE OF CONTENTS

What I Know About the Human Race

To see us—all of us, you can never allow your ideological blindfolds to be tied too tight. The ones handed to us, and the ones we acquire ourselves. It is, however, sometimes required of us, to let our old stories go.

ONE:
US

DREAMING IN THE TIME OF ISOLATION

A boy sleeps, and he dreams: He dreams of fear and he dreams of hell and he dreams of where he lives now and will forever more, and he dreams of the faces of his family burning in the long nights of these days now, and he dreams, too, of past worlds, the faces of men; the faces of the sons of men, covered in furs and skins and painted in the death of others, their hollowed eyes of broken glory coming hard on wild mounts from hell, their devil hooves pounding the earth in the name of all that have come before them.

He wakes and he screams and his father tells him, it'll be okay, and the boy, in his mind, backs away like some crab-like cave creature, his hands and feet scrambling amongst the scattered dreams of past plagues until backed against a weeping wall of fear and desolation.

He looks away—where? The blue of a dead screen, flickering, covering him, and he closes his eyes, and he says to himself, don't dream.

Next to him, in the dark of that same night, his younger sister, fearful in her time and lost to it, knows she, too, will dream, in the warmth of that room, her father with her and holding her—trying to, and she cries, tears she knows, tears she can't feel in these never-ending dreams of an echoing silence lost to the unforgiving vastness of a darkness everywhere. She wakes, a noise in the night, her brother next to her, and she looks to the window and her reflection there—falling, once again, into this endlessness of fear and desperation in the night.

The father, he covers her, his hand to her forehead, and he says, there there, now—now now, her fallen tears, the rattling of her fear chewing bones and soft tissue coming to him and settling heavy upon him. He leans forward and he whispers, it'll be okay, and she squeezes his hand and she closes her eyes and she waits—to flee, once again, a little girl on the back of duskywings.

And now the father, sitting upright next to his children, sleeps, and he, too, dreams, these dreams which are always dreams of long and empty streets in the night. Stopping, his heart pounding, resounding in his head, he watches thin pools of water gathered upon the road beginning to ripple. He looks behind him, an immeasurable distance back to the birthplace of darkness itself. He turns to run and a two-headed dog with massive jaws that foam and drip sink both sets of jaws deep into his face. He falls to the cobblestone surface of the road, his faceless head lulling forward, the dog's jaws taking it, fighting to enter his red dark hole. They hollow him out. They rip and consume the skin from his bones and they eat the bones so all that remains of him is a scull dripping in blood from a scalp that is nothing more than a few splotches of dark hair.

The children sleeping, the man wakes, covered in sweat, and in the dark, he whispers to himself, it'll be okay.

IN THIS LAND, THE AMERICAN POEMS

Raise Our Voices Up

What do you want me to say?
You're breaking my heart?
Fine, and what's that to you?
Wrap yourself in it and repair yourself,
Because at the end of all of this,
There's just:
Nowhere, alone, and coming fast—
Too fast.
Just don't,
Bring me all the things we might have been.
Bring me everything else.
Bring me—
Your courage.
Your voice.
Where? And is it coming back?
For only, if we would,

Raise your voice up.
But are we,
Too
Far
Down
The sloping shoulders of this world,
This particular dark hole of—
In this land of—
These yesterdays of—
What we could've been.
And yes, if only we would,
Raise our voice up.
But are we not, still—just,
Alone and holding on?
Where's the light of this enlightenment you said we could be?
But you bury it with you,
Don't you?
And yet,
We're better than all of that.
Better than all of that always.
Show me,
And I look around,
There—still: Tyre Nichols and George Floyd and …
Stop breaking my heart.
In this land of—

These yesterdays of—
What we could've been.
For only, if we would,
Raise your voice up,
We the people.
Otherwise,
We'll look around, where?
There—still: Tyre Nichols and George Floyd and …
Stop breaking my heart.

This House

We could sit on this porch and we could talk.
I wish we would.
In these,
Coming winds,
These,
Sunsets over yesterday hills,
Remembering:
Long lines of unmovable tall trees,
Sheltering us, in the coming of storms.
But for now, we'll sit and we'll talk,
Our view before us, our vision.
In the calmness we see how, and in the dark we ask why.
Of these moments now:
Hands laid upon us,
Tears falling,
Our finger to it,
Mine and yours.
But please, just stop and step back,
And come and sit with me,
On this porch,
In these,
Coming winds,
These,
Sunsets over yesterday hills,

Remembering:
This house now,
Behind us,
Mine and yours,
Burning.

QUITTING SMOKING

A tin drive-shed, two brothers, Jake and Jared, sitting on blocks of cracked white oak, drinking, passing time. Jake, turning to his younger brother, says, I wish ya could sew my mouth up.

Funny, replies Jared, I do too.

No, I mean it, I gotta quit these fuckin things. They're killin me.

If I sewed it up, how'd ya eat?

That's a good question.

You could use a straw.

Wouldn't work. If I could put a straw in there, I could put a smoke in there.

We could sew in good and tight.

A long workbench down the one side, an unused hoist in the center of the room. Posters of girls and cars.

Would ya do it?

What? asks Jared. Sew your mouth up?

Yeah.

Sure, I would, I guess, but it'll hurt like hell.

We got this whiskey, and I ain't feelin too much pain already. Ya got a needle?

I doubt it.

Any thread?

Thread wouldn't work, you could snap it too easy just opening your mouth.

Where's your fishing gear?

Right over there.

Well?

Well what?

We could use that.

Good idea. Let me get it.

Take your time.

What 'bout this one?

What 'bout one of them bigger bait hook ones?

This?

Yeah.

What pound line? Six or eight?

Better make it eight, I get powerful urges.

Let me thread it up. How's the whiskey?

Goin down good. Hey?

What?

When was the last time you used that hook?

I don't know, let me think. I caught that big bass on it, remember that?

Helluva fish.

Was.

I'm thinking though—

What's that?

Maybe we should sterilize it?

Probably should. Pass the lighter.

Here ya go.

How's this?

A little more, and Jake takes another sip of whiskey.

Ya think this is enough line?

Should be. What about a straw?

I dunno if we got one. I'll have a look.

Take your time, and Jake fires up a smoke.

Found one.

Great.

Ya ready.

Nope. Let me finish this last smoke.

I seen they had a boot drive on the bridge this morning.

Yeah, I got caught in it. I only had some change on me, but I had a couple boxes of new shells, and I gave em one of them.

Horrible thing, all them poor kids.

Fuckin crazy bastard. Gimme the straw.

Here ya go.

Is that a good spot?

More to the center.

Like that?

Yup. Better grip that chair, I don't want ya punching me.

I ain't gonna punch ya, just get it done.

All right, but damn this is gonna hurt.

Shit!

Hold still!

That hurt like a mother.

Take another drink.

Hold on, the straw. How's this?

Good.

I won't say a thing this time, I promise.

Ya better not and stay still.

There we go. That's a fine job if I don't say so myself. Here, let me get a rag, ya got a lot blood comin out of there.

That's better. Try and open your mouth.

Good, ya can't do it. Does it hurt?

What? You wanna drink? Hold on.

Here ya go, suck some up.

Look at that, works great.

What'ya doin now?

Why ya reaching for your smokes? Ya can't smoke, we sewed your mouth up.

My God, we didn't think about that. Did it just come to ya now?

What was the point of sewing your mouth up? Smoking through the straw like that? We need a smaller one, so your smoke won't fit in the end of it.

Ya look damn stupid, I'll can tell ya that.

Evening, boys—what the hell?

Oh, hey, Sugar.

My god, what have ya done?

What?

What the hell of ya done to Jake?

Nothing. He wanted to quit smokin.

Well, it don't seem to be workin so good, does it? He's smoking one now.

I know it. We need a smaller straw. Think we got one?

I don't know, hold on, I'll have a look.

THIS IS A CONVERSATION ON A TRAIN

Crazy, right?

Sorry?

The man lowers his paper. These mass shootings.

Oh, right. Yeah, crazy.

So many kids.

So wrong.

Lunatics with weapons. How's it make any sense at all?

It doesn't.

There's gotta be a way to keep guns out of crazy people's hands?

Define crazy?

What?

Crazy.

I don't know, someone who shoots up a classroom full of kids?

Were they crazy when they bought the gun?

Good question.

One in five people suffer from some form of mental illness.

Really?

Yeah.

That's a big number.

Less than five percent of the world's population owns nearly half of the world's privately held weapons. That's a big number.

A shit-ton of locked and loaded crazy.

Right.

What's the answer?

More guns and less mental healthcare.

What?

The answer, currently.

We're fucked.

Yup.

All right, well, this is me, good to see you.

Keep your head up.

No kidding.

Thoughts and prayers, brother.

You, too.

Whoa, what was that?

Train's stopped.

And now the lights?

In the church of comatose.

What?

Nothing.

Fuck, I'll be late.

Me too.

There's gotta be a way, don't you think?

How many more kids have to die?

Lots.

What?

Lots more will die.

It's hard to process that—hell, it's hard to believe this is even happening.

You have kids, right? Young ones?

Three and five.

When they throw a tantrum, what do you do, give in?

No, of course, not.

That's America right now.

A spoiled child with a gun?

Right. There's not a damn thing wrong with having to earn a right; a privilege, when it's been abused.

That could extend to more than a few things.

Political parties.

Sorry?

The whole red, blue, ad nauseam. I don't think I can go another day. It's fucking pathetic. Here, hold my beer and take my brain, I've checked out: I'm a Democrat, I'm a Republican. Configuring everything through a prism of a standing ideology. It makes no sense. Me against you.

What about looking at an issue, or a problem, and saying, what's the best solution, not for you and your personal gain, or that party of yours; your pathetic little get-ahead-ring-it-out club, but for everyone; the country, based on unencumbered, unbiased, free-thinking. Knowledge and facts. Honest intent. Instead of all this for sale thinking we have now. There's no integrity or accountability left, it's all bullshit.

Honest intent. I like that.

Go and ask Warren.

Meaningless, self-serving, self-righteous rhetoric.

Weaponized talking points: free markets, democracy, freedom, socialism, thank you for your service. We need to clear our brains out and move on. Reset. Or, as Wallace said, take a step back and challenge our default settings. Free markets? Really?

So, socialism?

Fuck socialism. Look, there's no such thing as a pure free market, and since that's true, which it is, and never will there be, it only leaves one thing, and that's getting the mix right. That's it. It's not rocket science. Capitalism. Socialism. Nothing but ideological concepts without any real practical purpose, other than telling people what they want or don't want to hear. Dividing people. What makes for a just society? That's the question. You want freedom? Democracy? There it is. The greater number of people that function and participate in a society, the greater the society becomes. It's the driver, and no amount of big business or big government can compensate for that. Shouldn't that be the purpose? Building a framework for the betterment of a nation? Allowing for the greatest opportunities for success, for everyone? But that necessitates a level playing field, which there isn't, not even close, look at the numbers. And so half the nation wants to re-elect, what?

A moron and a failed CEO president.

Social mobility, the ability to improve the standards of a nation's individuals, and by extension, society, have all gone out the window.

Serious neglect.

The thing about neglect is this, it always catches up. When special interest groups, lobbyists, donors, own your vote, what's left?

Not much.

You can make your mark next to red or blue, but when your elected official sets their course according to those that helped get them there, and help keep them there, they're not representing your voice, and the principle of 'we the people' is undermined, and by extension, democracy.

Self-serving swamp rats.

Greed and fuck-you politics. The American government needs to start by doing one thing, first and foremost, and immediately, and then moving out from there. It's imperative.

What's that?

Get off its knees and stop sucking corporate dick.

Well said.

There is no longer any certainty of uncompromised truth. Objectivity and the fundamentals have all been breached. The walls have come down. Everything is too big, the money too big.

Citizens United.

Yup, and it's washed out any integrity that was once there. Nearly a quarter of all American children live in poverty.

With a chance of being shot.

All too real and too sad. Do you think those kids care if you're wearing red or blue tie? Social protest, keeping the progressive card in your wallet valid, without real political and economic action, means what?

Not much.

Why do we allow this level of neglect? Why are we okay with that? Is it by design? It's hard not to see it that way. It can't just be ignorance, the cultural acceptance of antiquated and misleading thinking.

Political manipulation.

Why do we need them?

Who?

The political parties we have.

How would that work?

Everyone runs as an independent. No RNC. No DNC. Send the carpetbaggers packing. No special interest groups, lobbyists, corporate donations, Super Pacs. Only capped individual contributions, and that's it. Time to end the road show.

Take away the trough.

We need to ensure, as best as we can, the people's voice is being represented, and not some other agenda. And today, that is not happening, not even close. We take our minds back, and then the nation. Vote independent. Freeze the free-loading assholes out.

I like it.

You can have a house full of guns, it means what? You're free? Free-er? Without responsibility and accountability to others?

Fear.

Right. And they sell that shit hard and they sell it well.

Also too true and too sad. The whole damn thing is. When the hell is this train going to move? I'm late as hell.

When greed and self-interest take a seat.

So never.

Right.

We're fucked.

Yup.

ANNIE RIDES A BIKE

A little story of a little girl and here she goes: Keep your back straight, your balance right. Tiptoe tiptoe—oh, and there's a rock. Off the bike. "You're supposed to help me, Mom said."

Her brother, watching: "Ride your own bike."

On the bike—oh, and there's a car. Off the bike. Walk the bike. Never ride a bike near a car.

Tiptoe tiptoe, balance right, and here we—oh, and there's a cat. "Watch it, fat cat. I coulda run ya down." Old fat cat.

Her brother and his friends: "Scaredy cat. Scaredy cat."

Never mind them, we can do it. Right? Right. Ready? Ready. On the bike. Keep your back straight, your balance right. Tiptoe tiptoe—oh noooooo—

Her brother and his friends, laughing: "Don't cry, Annie. Maybe one day."

Her mother, asking: "Does it feel any better?"

"A little."

"Good, try get some sleep. I'll help you Saturday."

"Okay. Goodnight, Mommy."

"Goodnight, dear."

To her teddy bear in the dark: Can you see it there, little Angel Teddy? We can do it, can't we? Stupid boys. We hate 'em all, don't we?

On the bike.

Under the moonlight.

You go right in there, little Angel Teddy. We can do it, right? Right.

Ready? Ready. Keep your back straight, your balance right. Steer straight. Peddle peddle peddle. "Oh, look at us go, little Angel Teddy. Look at us go."

Keep your back straight, your balance right. Steer straight. Peddle peddle peddle.

And always, with the help of angels, too, of course.

Under the moonlight.

IN A SMALL TOWN (CALLED AMERICA): A ONE ACT PLAY

CHARACTERS

Jake Burleson: A large man, he works at the local mill, 34.

Jared Burleson: Shorter and thinner than his brother, repairs small engines and automobiles, 32.

Sugar: A tall, attractive blonde, married to Jake Burleson, 29.

PLACE

A tin drive-shed behind Jared Burleson's house, in a small mill town - Tidewater, the American south.

TIME

Present day.

Scene 1

SETTING: Interior, JARED BURLESON'S drive-shed. There's a grease-stained fridge, two blocks of white oak in front of an airtight stove. A garbage can surrounded by empty auto part boxes, dirty rags, discarded bottles and cans. On the walls are posters of cars and girls. An empty hoist in the center of the room, a long workbench.

AFTERNOON: JAKE and JARED are sitting on the blocks of white oak, each with a beer in their hand.

JAKE

Things are looking up.

JARED

Seems like it.

JAKE

I mean, once things are great again, things'll be lookin up.

JARED

Right.

JAKE

Oh, and by the way, I got my tests back.

JARED

Yeah?

JAKE

Doc said I'm shootin blanks.

JARED

Shit, Jake. I'm sorry to hear that.

(He gets up and grabs two more beers and sits back down, handing one to Jake.)

Have ya told Sugar?

JAKE

Last night.

JARED

How'd that go?

JAKE

'bout as good as you'd think. Ya know how much she wants kids. Not that I don't—I mean, you got your two and they're doin okay, right?

JARED

Right.

JAKE

Thing is, I don't wanna adopt some stranger's baby and say it's mine. Sugar don't neither. We could get her artificially knocked up, but—

JARED

What?

(JAKE shrugs and takes a sip of Beer.)

JARED

They got DNA.

JAKE

I know they got DNA, but nothin's perfect.

JARED

I guess.

JAKE

And then you're just—

JARED

So what'ya thinkin?

JAKE

(Looking at JARED, he takes a sip of beer.)

I want you to do it.

JARED

You what?

JAKE

You heard me.

JARED

Are you askin me to fuck Sugar?

JAKE

Yup.

JARED

Really?

JAKE

Yup.

JARED

Have you lost your goddamn mind?

JAKE

(Lifting his John Deere ball cap and Scratching the top of his balding head.)

Nope.

JARED

Does Sugar know?

JAKE

We talked about it.

JARED

You talked about it?

JAKE

Yup.

JARED

And what'ya think, Alice is just gonna be okay with me walkin next door and havin a go with Sugar? Cause I got news for ya, she won't be.

JAKE

She don't gotta know.

JARED

What'ya mean she don't gotta know? How the hell is she not gonna

know?

JAKE

Cause we ain't gonna tell her, that's how.

JARED

For fuck's sake, this is nuts, Jake. I can't fuck Sugar.

JAKE

What'ya mean you can't fuck Sugar? She looks good still. Hell,

she's a lot better lookin than that girl you were fuckin back

in high school.

JARED

She wasn't that bad.

JAKE

The hell she wasn't.

JARED

C'mon, Jake, get serious, you don't mean this shit?

JAKE

I'm as serious as the day is long, little brother. Hell, it

won't take more than a time or two. Didn't ya always tell me

all you had to do to knock up Alice was to hang your pants on

the bed post?

JARED

True enough, but still—

JAKE

At least this way the kid'll be a Burleson.

(He finishes his beer and throws the empty at the garbage can.)

Besides, ya don't gotta worry 'bout a thing. We'll just get up a little early, you walk to my place and I'll come here. After you're done, you come back here like nothing ever happened, and I'll head back home.

(He stands.)

Think about it.

(He walks to the door and looks back.)

Oh, and by the way, Sugar says she'll be droppin eggs in the next day or two.

JARED

She'll be what?

JAKE

That's what she said.

JARED

You talked about it?

JAKE

Yup, we talked about it. Later.

JARED

Yeah, later.

(BLACKOUT)

(END OF SCENE)

Scene 2

SETTING: Interior drive-shed. JARED, standing at his workbench, working on a motor part.

MORNING: JAKE enters. He walks to the fridge and grabs a beer.

JAKE

How'd it go?

(JARED looks back.)

JAKE

Ya got it done, right?

JARED

Yeah, I got it done, but I had to turn her around.

JAKE

What? Why?

JARED

What'ya mean why?

JAKE

Whatever, as long as you got it done.

JARED

Maybe cause she's your wife, or somethin like that. What'ya think?

JAKE
How long ya been married?

JARED
Eleven years.

JAKE
Do ya love her still?

JARED
What? Yeah, I guess. How the hell am I supposed to know?

JAKE
It's hard to know, ain't it?

JARED
Yeah, it's not easy.

JAKE
Ya think she still loves you?

JARED
Of course, she does. Why wouldn't she?

JAKE
I didn't say she didn't. What about Sugar?

JARED
What about her?

JAKE
Think she still loves me?

JARED

Hell, I don't know. Why?

JAKE

It's just something ya wonder about, ya know? That's all. It's not like it's not possible. It happens all the time.

JARED

I guess.

JAKE

Do ya think it matters?

JARED

What?

JAKE

Love.

JARED

I don't know—for fuck's sake, Jake.

JAKE

(He tosses his empty at the garbage can.)

I think it does.

(He walks to the door and looks back.)

We should try again tomorrow, while things are goin' good.

JARED

Goin' good?

JAKE

Yeah, you know, with the eggs.

JARED

Right, later.

(BLACKOUT)

(END OF SCENE)

Scene 3

SETTING: Interior drive-shed. JARED is standing at his workbench cleaning a motor part.

AFTERNOON: SUGAR enters and walks to the fridge and grabs a beer. She opens it and looks at a calendar on the wall with a picture of a girl draped over the hood of a car.

SUGAR

They make good money, ya know.

(She sips her beer.)

It's not just the money, it's the connections. Ya know that, right?

(She walks to the workbench and pulls herself onto a high metal stool. She crosses her legs, her one foot bouncing.)

I suppose ya talked about it?

JARED

Not much we did.

SUGAR

What'd he say?

JARED

He wanted to know if it went okay.

SUGAR

And?

JARED

And what?

SUGAR

What'ya say?

JARED

Not much.

SUGAR

Not much?

JARED

Nope. Can we not talk about this?

SUGAR

Why don't ya wanna talk about it?

JARED

What's the point?

SUGAR

The point?

(She uncrosses her legs and crosses them the other way, her foot starting to bounce again.)

Why's it gotta be so hot in here? What's wrong with that damn fan?

(She leans forward.)

The point is, we need to figure this out, and right this goddamn minute we do.

JARED

(He grabs a rag and begins to wipe his hands.)

What's with you?

SUGAR

Did ya not hear us last night? I'd be surprised if ya didn't.

JARED

A little, I did.

(He walks to the fridge and grabs a beer.)

What was up?

SUGAR

I told him, I ain't no puppy-mill slut, and I ain't sleeping with you no more.

JARED

You're what?

SUGAR

What?

(They look at one another.)

JARED

You ain't sleeping with me no more?

SUGAR

Of course, I am, I just ain't doin it for him no more.

JARED

That makes no sense.

SUGAR

Are you dumb? There's a world of difference between my wanting to sleep with you and him wanting me to. And I can tell you this much, we had better figure this out, and I mean now.

JARED

(Leaning against the workbench, he sips his beer.)

How long we been together?

SUGAR

I don't know, a couple of years. Why?

JARED

In all that time we been doin it, were ya never worried about getting pregnant? Or were ya just hoping ya would and say it was Jake's?

SUGAR

Ya don't get it, do you? All this damn talk of babies, I can hardly take it.

JARED

What'ya mean?

SUGAR

(She put her beer down and gets up and begins to pace in her flip-flops.)

It's the last thing I'm ever gonna do, do understand that?

JARED

What?

SUGAR

This world is a hard world, Jared Burleson, and it gets no easier being a woman, that's for damn sure. And if you think I'm gonna get dropped down another rung or two by having either yours or your brother's damn babies, ya gotta another thing comin. Besides, it plays absolute havoc with your body, destroys it completely. Is that what you want?

JARED

Hold on, Sugar, are you telling me all this time you've been on birth control?

SUGAR

That is correct, smart boy, yes I have.

JARED

And all this time Jake thought you were trying to get pregnant?

SUGAR

Correct.

JARED

And then it turns out, he's sterile? What would ya have done if he hadn't been?

SUGAR

I don't know. I'd of figured somethin out.

JARED

And now he's got me doin ya to get ya pregnant even though I already am and you're on birth control?

SUGAR

(Sitting back up on the stool.)

As it turns out, yes.

JARED

(Pushing himself off the workbench he stands in front of Sugar.)

You're somethin, Sugar. I don't know what, but you're definitely somethin.

(The small fan in the window begins to rattle, blowing warm sticky air.)

JARED

(Reaching his hands past Sugar to the workbench, he leans into her.)

Sugar.

SUGAR

I know, baby.

(She turns and looks out the window.)

Let's just go.

(BLACKOUT)

THE END

We walk often in our remembering, but so, too, must we walk in the honest intent of our truth now. Or, at least try to ...

TWO:
LOVE

RIVER POOL

There's a river I go to. I stand and I watch, wondering, the warming sun holding me, saying, oh, this eternity of your days, your tortured heart, the hardest heart. I look to the dark pool of water, and it frightens me. A river pool. The uncertainty of its darkness, its imagined depth. And yet, I'm drawn to it, looking for what? Why? These dark waters reaching to the desperation of my thoughts here in the middle of where? A nowhere meant for what? And it seems to me, even it does not know; is not aware, of the power it holds—the current of the river avoiding it, skirting around it, and I'd jump into these dark waters, under these forever skies, if I could just see my way to not trusting myself, but I do, still, at least, to the very end of what that means to me, I do, and it calls again from the depth of its dark waters, a voice that is not a voice sounding and resounding within me, saying: Come, swim, in me. I am water. And I think, even this dark pool of water is frightened of its own self, I can see it in its reflection. A thrill is just a thrill and need not be anything more. Is that true? I wonder, and I think of that story, the one everyone knows, of that girl—and she was just thirty-nine with a flash of rust-colored hair who jumped into this river pool of dark water and was never seen again. Her story, it's stayed with me—is it her voice I hear calling to me? Of course, it is, her clutched fingers reaching. Why? Does she see the same desperation within me? To jump? To Swim? In dark water? My sorrow? Is that what she sees? And I hear her, half-winking, telling me life can be again the goodness of an unfaltering self, safe and promising, and she dances; water dancing to the unseen rhythm of a certain sadness, the kind bred from never being freed of a remembered desire; never again able to walk—in what? Not water.

Is she there, still? Listening? Watching? Seeing? Trapped as she is, in these dark waters; the eternity of her yesterdays. The once tallness of her bent and twisted to the unknowing of everything beyond her dark water; beyond her not seeing? Why'd she do it? "A wicked flu?" And then, "My love." Who's she saying this to? Me? Or is it just another thought surfacing from the depth of what once was? Come, never mind that, she says, come now to the slow comforting movement of my dark water. A place to hide; a place to trick yourself from the world, not just mine. Not just yours. And what am I to do? Jump? Should

I? Like her? I look to the steady flowing river avoiding the dark pooling of water calling to me: Trust me.

Can I? And I ask myself: What is real and what is imagined?

And what of the others? The ones before? The ones now and the ones that shall come? All in need—wanting, of your dark water?

You are not the only one, I say to the unseen her, a breeze picking up and carrying my words over the open spaces between us; beneath this warming sun; these forever skies, that I shall not forsake.

I no longer go there—that river pool. Those dark waters. But I do, from time to time, wonder, is she there still, dancing; water dancing to the unseen rhythm of—and I stop myself, and ask: Did she ever know—does she know yet, the unused spaces of time between us; beneath this warming sun; these forever skies of a tortured heart.

The hardest heart of all.

I DON'T CARE IF YOUR EYES ARE GREEN

Neil Young is playing, 1971 Neil Young on a stage just him Neil Young. Massy Hall. The BBC. I'm at the kitchen table, my legs crossed, a coffee. Your downstairs cleaning up, you. The other day I read a story you wrote, your aunt was trying to put a snowsuit on this young you in this story set in a vast, isolated North, and it didn't go so well, according to what you wrote. You rebelled—a meltdown, because, well, fashion. Because, well, a girl just wants to be seen. And I saw that last night (was it that little girl there with me?) on our walk by the lake a car coming snow drifting crazy-like in its headlights. "There's a car coming," I said, and you moved more to the center of the road, and you said, "It's still far yet." But it wasn't.

And right now, Neil is singing, "Lullabies in your eyes." My eyes, your eyes—all of our eyes, because that's the thing, isn't it? Days that are those days that just won't be days gone now: these lullabies in our eyes. A lullaby, or a screaming? Either way, here still, like a car coming at night snow drifting crazy-like in its headlights.

But that's all right, all of it, I know it is, because your heart is not a vast, isolated North, snow drifting crazy-like, no.

And so, take my hand.

Why?

Because that's what someone told me once; what people do, when they start out together on a new beginning.

Charlie?

Yeah, of course, sort of.

And we're here now, building these days now, at night by a lake the snow drifting crazy-like and we say—fuck it, let them be lullabies in someone else's eyes, and all that screaming, too. And I say, yes, all I need is yours, in these days of days that will be our days and not yesterday's days one day, and I don't even care if they're green. Do you?

IN THE LONG NIGHTS NOW

In the long nights the longer yet that come still find me still wondering, with you. Where were you? And you say, free (but bound eternally). A trap in your mind feeding. And I say—show me, take me down to that downtown, the broken bricks and cracked mortar one, the graffiti not fading one, where it's always written, Survivors, and where Jimmy Dean dreams were never really dreams and only ever the one by one falling of packaged 60s slogans like some Joan Didion, Anaïs Nin nightmare—you re-pointed with words—this sanctity, searching for that eternity, a name drifting onto a piece of paper, a song replaying, the trap in your mind feeding, in the long nights the longer yet that come still find me still wondering, with you.

Where were you? And you say, that place, you know the one, where I sometimes live, so unknowing of myself, a place of aisles and longer drives, of non-messages and midnight parks by the water, and too, remembering—not you, the ringing in of a new year—that one: "Ring Out,

Wild Bells!" and from there, where? Well, tomorrow, against the chaos, of course. And what of lost together in that place that is the enactment of our words; words you know; words, too, in need of being found again in the long nights the longer yet that come still find me still wondering, with you.

THESE NIGHTS IN MONTREAL

His wife died. Since then, he's done this twice. I'm not sure why.

A resolution? Remembrance? An understanding?

I watched him: Sometime in February walking alone at night the cold dark streets of Montreal, and I wondered, what's lost—what's to be found, within the eternity of a single night?

He looked to the old three and four story brick and mortar apartments, the ones he liked, and in the quiet of that night, I heard him say, are you happy? Content? In love? The past not there and stealing today?

He walked on, past the old Forum—Montreal glory days, and then downtown, just big enough and not scattered and not lost with just enough to read between the lines, like the hotels, the old ones, not so much the new ones: Le Nouvel Hôtel. And I wanted to say to him, is it not just another day—another middle of the night trying not to know?

He walked beneath the large Crescent Street mural of Leonard Cohen, his hands in his pockets, and he looked up, and he said, people, it's always people, seeking their Saturday night-like validation.

Leonard looked at him, and he said, Hallelujah, and he tipped his hat.

The man now, he looked to the darkness, the covering of it, and he walked to it, just there on the edge of downtown where it waited and it called and fuck romancing that, call it what it is, what it always has been: blood dripping from the reaching of our cold dark fears and called something else.

This duplicity, of us.

A small, nondescript brick building. A red door. A place not anywhere—and everywhere, feeding on itself like some truth that isn't one rationalized to become one. A conversation you said you never had. An action you said you don't have. I recalled a lyric from that time, "I ain't lookin for nothin, from anyone's eyes." And she had said, oh my shame.

My shame.

He entered. A large doorman in a dark suit nodded, and he walked up the steep stairs, French plume glass wall sconces lighting the way, his shoes leaving a dusty trail of snowy prints on the red carpet amongst the shadows in a place where shadows moved only in the dark.

A kind of place—the kind of quiet, old money required: paneled walls, Persian rugs, and coffered ceilings. He checked his coat with the young girl there and walked to the bar. A middle-aged bartender with a crisp white shirt and black tie. Expensive brands of booze lining the shelves behind the bar.

Irish, he said, and he took a seat. There was another man at the other end of the bar and they looked at one another and they did not speak.

It was a waiting room type-place and there was a door and he looked at that door.

He sipped his whiskey, and he said, I've only ever seen someone walk out that door twice. But I know what's back there. Not that I've ever been, but I know.

The words, she's back there, drifting in the dark places of his brain, lingering and rattling and lingering some more.

He asked the bartender, is she?

The bartender didn't answer, he wasn't allowed to, privacy—secrecy, of the utmost importance in a place like that.

It was a woman, he continued, with a masquerade mask held in front of her face. He looked back at that door and took another sip of whiskey. Shame is believing we're flawed and unworthy of love. Belonging, too. And I know it, and I know it from her.

The dark. The dark we reach to. The dark we want. At least, some do. Like a need. You don't know me but maybe you do?

Maybe you want to?

All the endless reasons, and yet, perhaps they could all meet at one place, these reasons, and become one thing, because what does need want shame help mean as one word?

The only other person was a man, he continued, without his face covered, like some burning-eyed child of the dark. Uncomfortable to look at, but an attraction, too, for some, I guess. And most likely, that was the trouble, or at least, part of it.

Why was he here? She's dead. And what's that one word? And at what point does a person's truth stop being a lie?

When it needs to be.

Or, it doesn't, because you can live with what you know, the gales of your mind under the gathering of darkening clouds, your compass now.

He was staring off nowhere, a place we've all been, and he put his glass on the bar and the bartender asked if he'd like another one? He looked at the bartender, at his own sadness he saw there; the bartender's pity.

"I ain't lookin for nothin, from anyone's eyes." Maybe that's it? The answer. She felt she could only ever be seen in the dark—in the unknown of the dark? We all hold pain differently, but—call it what you want, it was real, and it was there, and it was waiting.

The man stood and walked to the coat check, and as he waited, he looked back at that door. Is he hoping she'll walk out from there and see him? The impossibility of that? A man available to her that wasn't in the dark but is now? A man now, too, from her past? Does the dark hide the past or set it free?

He took his coat from the girl and thanked her and he walked back down the stairs. He walked again the cold dark city streets of Montreal, and he looked again at the old hotels—these cathedrals holding our wanting: time, here, now, and never time gone. He looked at the old three and four story brick and mortar apartment buildings, and he asked again, are you happy? Content? In love? The past not there and stealing today?

Standing beneath a streetlight on the quiet Boulevard de Maisonneuve I looked up at his apartment and through a window and I watched him take his coat off and walk to the living room. I watched him pick up a framed picture of his wife, and as he reached his finger to it, touching it, I thought of the hope they must have once held called always. He put the picture back and remained standing until the sun came up, no longer cold and alone in the dark.

Sometime in February, in Montreal.

The eternity of a single night.

Her words—our words, there and with us still, oh my shame.

My shame.

THE EARLY POEMS, PART ONE

Is There a Question, She Needed to Know

Who is searching,
Here among us,
The not familiar, unknown, perhaps, not preferred?
And if there's a question,
Ask it in kerosene shadows, snow falling,
In the mountains, away from here.
And will they see,
The games played,
The bruise of a knee,
A shirt-tail dancing?
Find your question,
Hold it, and ask it,
Effortless and free.
She kept these poems for me,
And among the typed words,
The not familiar, unknown, perhaps, not preferred,
Was there a question,
She needed to know?

Come Whisper to Me

How I feel is what I see,
Which is what I wrote,
So I must have meant it,
And yet,
Just what was it,
That I was feeling?
Fearful, and in too deep,
So often, it says here,
Dreaming of visions,
Of comfortable spaces,
Screaming.
Among these words,
I try and remember,
But cannot,
So come and whisper to me,
So I may see,
That which I was feeling,
Once again.

LOSS IN THE TIME OF LOVING

We walk in these gardens of stone, the reaching of graveyards from all our time, fixed, unmoving, rooted in the earth, each stone a marker of a remembered story, or perhaps, a story once remembered. Somewhere. For someone. And in the gardens of new life, rooted in the earth of here and now, we have among us our shared stories, stories that are always told with the eyes. It is a covenant we all must make, to walk both: Loss in the time of loving. And in my time, I have had a story, remembered in each day's new dark, thinking: How many more will there be? Opportunities of seeing in your eyes this story of us, the one more than just what we went through, you and the other kids, and is, most certainly, a telling, of all our time, together.

We had a farm of many acres at the back of which was a hardwood patch where I would take down tall trees in the warm months with the pickup and the dog and the sounds of turkeys trying to flee with their too small wings—hickory, beech, maple, and oak, mostly. It was hot work and it was good work and I liked it. There was a day, an exceptionally hot day, with the big trees falling, I looked up and you were there parked on your little pink and white bike with a bottle of water in your basket. Your five-year-old face, where I was certain, all that was good in the world lived, was red, for why would it not have been? You'd ridden and walked that little bike of yours from our old stone farmhouse down the back laneways and over and over acres—at least seventy, of irrigated corn fields, to bring that bottle of water to me. I smiled and we didn't say a word and the dog joined us back from scenting and chasing things that live in forests. The three of us. Like so many other days. The bigger kids at school, my mornings at my desk, afternoons with you. And the dog. Off we'd go. It didn't matter so much where. I put my hand to your head that day and smiled again and said, thank you. It's hot, you told me. Yes, I replied, and we shared the water, our eyes building this story of us, remembered now by me; remembered one day by you, a stone as its marker, as you walk in that garden, the one that is a covenant we all must make: Loss in the time of loving.

When reaching to your fate residing in the folds of time, beware the risks inherent to this, and so, call to it if you must, but remember, as Jim Harrison said, "Beware, O wanderer, the road is walking too." And as Sheila Watson said, "When you fish for the glory you catch the darkness too."

THREE: TIME & FATE

IN NORTH HATLEY

The mighty Rivière Massawippi, and it's moving, ice flowing to the edges of it, the silhouette of the mountain beyond it, stripped, naked trees, and I want to climb it.

I look and I can see us surfacing from the river, and you look back. Why? I'm not. I'm looking at the clean, unbroken lines of undisturbed snow. My foot behind me, moving forward, and I look at you and tell you, come, step here, in the future with me.

You don't know, and you say, are we?

Yes.

You look down, and I say, no, there. The clean, unbroken lines of undisturbed snow.

My foot moving forward, breaking—smashing, and I say to you, you walk too, for we can be survivors—not survivors of a future that never happened, no, not that, you say, and I say, no, never that.

In the coming night you'll dance, me watching, remembering, and you'll ask, does it make sense? Any of it?

Does it have to?

I've been back there—used, hard, and taken, and here I am now, and I am what? Running naked, away from the cold moving darkness of the river, screaming, crying.

These prints we leave, visible only for a few days, then gone.

Are they?

You in my arms, shivering, the river flowing, and in that darkness, together we see the duplicity of love, time, and place.

Here in North Hatley, survivors of a future happening now.

TWENTY OR THIRTY GRAND

What'ya doin?

I thought it might be 24/7.

What'ya need?

Smokes.

I got some. On the dash. Grab me one. He watches her. Jesus Christ, he thinks.

She lights a cigarette and passes him the lighter and the smokes. What'ya doin? With that chain, I mean, what'ya doin?

He looks around at the 3 a.m. darkness.

She does too.

I'm takin the cash machine.

The what?

The ATM.

The whole machine?

Yeah.

For the money?

Why else?

Why don't ya just smash it and take the money?

Ya can't, they ain't built like that, otherwise, everyone would be walkin around smashin em, wouldn't they?

Aren't ya afraid you'll get caught?

Nope.

Why not? I would be. I don't think I could ever do somethin like that.

I've done it before.

You have?

Yup.

Lots of times?

Enough times.

How much money's in there?

I don't know. Twenty or thirty grand.

What if someone comes by?

You mean like you?

She doesn't answer and she toes out her cigarette. I won't say anything.

I know you won't.

They look at one another.

What's your name?

Daisy.

Daisy?

Yeah, Daisy Chainsaw.

That's a great name—wait, wasn't that a band?

Was, but they broke up, and it was available, so I took it.

All right, Daisy, time to step back, and he grabs a length of pipe from the back of the pickup and smashes out the door glass.

No alarm sounds and he knocks away the larger jagged pieces holding to the frame. He steps inside. Pass me the chain.

She does, and staying bent over, she watches him wrap the chain around the cash machine. That's it? That's all there is to it?

Yup, and he walks back out the door opening. Smash and grab.

The American way.

They hear a car.

Fuck. He takes her arm and they kneel and together they watch the car approaching. It's a cop, and he starts to unhook the chain from the truck. She sees a gun tucked into the waist of his pants. If they come this way, you can either run, or jump in with me, your choice.

The cruiser stops, white-blue tailpipe smoke drifting in the early morning dark.

He looks at Daisy. Well?

I should at least know your name.

Jay.

Really?

Yeah, why?

No reason. What about the money?

What about it?

You're just gonna leave it?

There's other money.

There is?

There's no shortage of cash machines.

No, I guess that's right. We could try another one, it's early yet.

The cop steps out of the car, shining a flashlight.

He looks at Daisy. You should go, while you got the chance.

They watch the cop walking toward them, the light upon them growing stronger.

Daisy looks at Jay. I'll stay, if that's all right?

Ya sure about it?

We could hook the chain back on the truck, and we could just drive away. He's not in his car, and maybe like, you could ram his cruiser.

He looks at Daisy.

It might work.

He pulls the gun out from the back of his pants. So might this.

She hooks the chain back on the truck. Let's just go.

The cop calls out, step out where I can see you. I ain't fuckin around, it's too damn early, and it's too damn cold.

He looks at Daisy. Ready?

Yeah.

Stay low, and when you get in the truck, stay down.

She nods.

All right then, and they make a break for the doors.

What the hell, the cop says, and he aims his gun. What the fuck are you doin?

Sitting low in the front seat, Daisy watches Jay drop the truck into gear. He hits the gas, the tires grabbing gravel, the backend fishtailing.

Shit, the cop says, and he starts to shoot, bullets piercing the windshield, the cash machine busting out the front door and the window—glass exploding, the machine bouncing and launching into the air.

Jay looks at Daisy, and he smiles, and as he looks back, he takes a bullet to the forehead.

Daisy's eyes widen, and she looks back at the cop. She reaches her foot to the brake and hits it, the truck stopping, the cash machine rolling and bouncing, flying over the truck and taking out the cop. Oh, fuck, she says. She puts the truck in park and looks at Jay. We didn't see that comin, did we? She leans over him and opens the door, and as she does, a Taco Bell wrapper falls from the truck. She leans back and says, it was nice meeting you, Jay, but it's time for you to go, and she kicks him out. She closes the door and drops the truck into gear. She turns the radio on and it's George Michael singing Freedom, and she laughs, tapping the steering wheel, and she begins to sing: *All we have to do now / Is take these lies and make them true somehow / All we have to see Is that I don't belong to you /And you don't belong to me* ... She looks in the rear-view mirror, at the two dead bodies, the cash machine bouncing and rolling behind her, and she turns the radio up, driving into her better days now, singing, *freedom.*

TIME IS A LAZY, SHADED RIVER

In the 1,000 Island district of the St. Lawrence River, I took a stroll wanting to stretch my legs. I came upon a young boy and an old man fishing, and I smiled, thinking of my own time as a young boy fishing on the banks of a river with my grandfather. A warm breeze picked up, and I remembered my grandfather staring at the current, watching, as I was certain he was, his time drifting before him on that lazy, shaded river, real and gone, and there again, for him to pluck at and say—see, it's right there, still all right there, when I was just a boy, like you. And in this, there would be contentment, without meaning, in the honest days of a life—and the days, too, I witnessed, that young boy, six, maybe seven, wanting to climb up through the worn buttonholes of his time.

Thirty-eight million people, I remember him saying, staring at the current of the river. I didn't know then, as I do now, he meant the second world war, and all the people that had died in the name of fascism, the current riding over the backs of those dead, like it was the dead of the first world war, in the days of his youth. His days, too, as a young man on the heels of trade union bashing, the collapsing of markets, the Great Depression. The current riding over all of it, indestructible, eroding rocks, like the obstacles placed in its path by the hands of us. He looked at me, and he said, it's always been there, never-ending, and it never will not be. What, I asked? A simple and known thing. A constant, he said. I waited. Our needing—reaching, to a just society.

Yesterday Germany, today America, and tomorrow, most certainly it will be somewhere else, but none of that will ever stop the current of our need of a just society, flowing as it does, still, over the backs of the dead.

One of which now is his.

CASH, GUNS, BOOZE AND WHORES: DESPERATION NEVER WINS

It was a failed attempt.

We needed to keep going.

I'm a boy peddling a bike hard down a gravel road toward a distant world of my own making.

And see me now, at the world's largest airport terminal—arrested.

South Korea.

Did you know there were entire worlds beneath these conduits to other places? Detention centers, interrogation rooms, law-enforcement offices, a prosecutor's office, a court room and judge, and boom, just like that, from jail to guilty and on an Interpol list.

I had been caught leaving the country with twenty grand in cash–yeah, I know, a big mistake, and one I would not normally make, but the night before had been a late one, and I had been rushing to make my flight.

What's four grand among friends, pay the fine and move on.

Problem was, I was on my way to Russia, and I still had sixteen grand, six more than I was legally allowed to travel with, and now, having missed my flight, I had to loop through Hong Kong to get to Moscow – two more international lines to cross.

I could either find someone in line and ask them if they'd mind holding six grand for me as we cleared customs, or I could start stuffing cash in all my things.

I surveyed the other passengers on the plane—who?

She seemed nice, but not too nice, and we started chatting. I explained I had come into twenty grand while in Korea and the problems I was having travelling with it, and would she mind holding six of it while we cleared customs?

Twenty percent? Wtf? I was starting to feel like Hemingway's fish. Fifteen.

Seventeen, five.

Fine.

Cash, guns, booze and whores.

Russia.

Black Land Rovers and E-Series BMWs with drivers with guns and a beautiful girl.

I'd met up with the others, a former World's Strongest Man—a hard-ass, when he wanted to be, and a giant Scottish man, tipping the scales at well over four hundred pounds, a PhD in geology, and drinking, and world class at that, no matter where we were, Asia, South America, Iceland, the Baltic states, the Eastern Bloc, and of course, Russia. He could put away twenty or thirty ounces of vodka and a half dozen beers—have a safe night boys, and off he'd go to bed. And only one time did I see him miss the elevator and walk into the wall. He was a good friend, and I miss him still.

Lunch in a Japanese restaurant—and now we're not, we're in a backroom behind a steel door without handles. And there he was, with two women, his arm around the one, talking to me through his representative, 'Natasha'. And behind him? Let's just call him—well, you didn't call him anything. He seemed all right, for what he was, which was what? Never far from the man.

That night.

In a nightclub owned by him, like so many other things, other clubs, restaurants, magazines, every billboard in Moscow. A Putin trickle down friend, or so we'd come to learn later. The next time I saw him, I was in Columbus, Ohio. He thought he'd come and take in an event. He was greeted by the FBI and detained for seventy-two hours, just because they could, just to let him know they knew who he was and that he was there.

Later.

Three in the morning later—and you want to do what? Pile in the cars with the drivers, the guns, the girls, and head out of the city to the woods and drink vodka and shoot deer with handguns?

What'd I do?

I drank the vodka, popped a few rounds and thought of Hunter.

Sunday Morning.

Red Square and it hit home. I was feeling a little under the weather and lagging behind Natasha and the hard-ass from steel-town, UK. I rounded a corner and was swarmed by a pack of street kids holding up fur hats for sale and looking to pickpocket me. Natasha turned around and yelled his name and that was it, they scattered. That's when I knew, steel-town, too, we looked at one another, and we could tell we were saying the same thing to ourselves at the same time: Fuck.

It was Sunday, and Lenin's tomb was closed. It didn't matter. Natasha talked to the guard and that was it, in we went.

All in all, none of this turned out so well. Surprising? It shouldn't have been, but there was no, all is right in Oz. No, Dorothy get me home. Desperation never wins.

THAT DAY WE PLAYED BINGO IN FLORIDA

It would seem impossible to live a life without understanding just how big a role the random acts of life play in the outcome of who we become, or for that matter, that we're even here still—that you haven't been shot; that you somehow walked away from an accident you had no business walking away from; that you haven't been eaten by pigs; that you have all your limbs; that you haven't been arrested, and are still behind bars. Okay—so, those are some of mine, and I'm sure you have your own. I'll highlight one, simply because it was the first time I became aware of the unexplained randomness of life, and a thing called karma.

I was twelve and we were on a family vacation in Clearwater, Florida, along with my best friend and his family. A beach motel and a scheduled day at Marineland, a big deal in the mind of a twelve-year-old. It was time to get ready, and ... I couldn't find my wallet, with the money

I had saved for the trip, twenty, possibly twenty-five dollars, that in the 70s, had real purchasing power. Soon, everyone was helping to look for it, but, nope, it was gone . Up against having to leave, Jake (my father) pulled me aside, and said, "You need to learn to be more aware, to take better care of your things, especially when it comes to money, and so, I have no choice but to tell you, you can't come." It was a big blow, but then, if he'd allowed me to come, without my money, he would have had to pay for me, and that wasn't happening. My best friend, being my best friend, said, "I'll stay back with you." We watched the others leave, and we had the day to ourselves.

After spending the morning at the beach, we walked back to the motel to see what was up, and head to our rooms to get something to eat. While in the lobby, we noticed a bingo game was about to start, and we inquired how to join. I think the fee was around two-fifty, and my friend paid for us both. And there we were, two twelve-year-old kids, our bingo cards ready, and I remember looking around and noticing that the next youngest person in the room was a good fifty or sixty years older than we were. A sea of blue hair. The prize money was bigtime—fifty dollars. We were focused and we were ready and I won. I couldn't believe it, and yet, I made enemies that day, these much older people, for the rest of my stay, shaking their heads at me with utter disgust whenever they saw me. My friend and I were thrilled—I'd doubled my money and was thanking Jake for it. After all, if it hadn't been for his 'punishment,' we wouldn't have won the bingo jackpot. I paid my friend back the entry fee, and noticing a diner across the street, said, let's go.

At this point in my life, I had never been to a diner on my own, and wasn't really sure how the whole thing worked, but we figured out, and ordered way too much food, of course, with my friend reaching back to the booth behind him and helping himself to the not finished Budweiser bottles left behind. We were celebrating. On the way out, we noticed abandoned money on tables, tips, they were called, I learned later, but in real time at that point, I had no idea, and figured, man, I was on a roll.

It was this day, at the age of twelve, I learned, not only about the randomness of life, but about a thing called karma. I had picked up something in the ocean and was violently ill for the next two or three days. And, of course, someone had seen us pocketing the abandoned diner money and walking back to the motel with it, and reported us. We caught hell: We couldn't leave the motel, and now not only were the older people looking at us sideways, so too was everyone else on the trip with us. We had to return to the diner and repay the money, with a premium, while offering an apology to the staff. I had taken a big net gain and worked it back to less than what

I'd lost, still minus the Marineland trip. It was a vacation filled with lessons: Don't push your luck, ignorance is never a good thing, karma is real, and most importantly, avoid taking older people's bingo money, the looks alone are never worth it.

THE WITCH IN THE WOODS

Across a busy road at the edge of a new subdivision was a forest, and in that forest was an old house.

Trees and bushes overgrown, the grass wild with weeds.

An intimidating place, full of mystery and wonder, especially if you were a young girl or boy growing up across the road on the quiet streets of a new subdivision.

Why wouldn't they sell?

Hidden away and rundown like that?

What kind of life is that?

A mad, crazy woman.

A witch.

Worse even.

You think so?

Oh, possibly, much worse.

Alice was with all the other children. She was one of the smallest ones, with red hair and a face full of freckles.

It was a rite of passage to be the one, and she was determined to be that one.

They had been there for over an hour, after their supper, all of them saying they'd be the one to do it, and yet, no one had moved. They hadn't dared to.

"Let's do it together?" said one of the kids.

Each one waiting for the other one. No one moved. It was almost dark now, and who would do it then?

"I'll go," said Alice, and she stood.

"You, Alice?"

The others laughed.

"Why not, me? I'm not afraid."

"She'll eat you alive."

"You're no bigger than a button."

Alice put her hands on her hips and looked at the group. "Stay here and wait. I'll show you."

They couldn't believe it. Alice?

"Don't forget about them bushes," one of kids said.

"Oh God, yeah, that's right, Alice. Don't forget about them bushes. She'll have ya for sure then, cold with your blood still warm."

"Think that's real?" asked Alice.

"Of course, it is."

"Everyone knows it is."

"There's only one spot in and out that's safe."

"All the other thorns are tipped with poison. Wait and see all the bones of dead squirrels and things."

"We could do it tomorrow," said Alice's best friend, Liv, the only other girl in the group. "I'd come with ya, then."

"Nope, it's now or never," said Alice. "I'm goin and I'm not afraid."

"Don't forget to bring back a little silver bell, or it won't count," said one of the boys.

"Jimmy, where'd your brother say it was safe to pass through? Tell me again."

The only one in the history of the development to have made it back with a little silver bell. Jimmy's older brother, Tommy.

"To the left of the old walkway. That what he said. Said he got lucky."

Alice started on her way. She stopped and looked back. "Don't leave without me."

"We'll be right here."

"Promise?"

"We promise," said Liv.

"If we hear ya screamin," said one of the boys, "we'll go and get help."

"Thanks," said Alice, and she turned around and started walking.

She worked her way slowly through the woods, stopping and listening.

An old owl called.

She looked up and she wished the moon was bigger, the day less cloudy.

She stood behind a large oak tree, peeking out at the house. There were lights on in the house. A porch light.

She waited longer, and not seeing anyone moving in the house, she stepped out from behind the tree and walked crouched over toward the house.

She made it to the bushes and crouched down more. There were no sounds. She couldn't see anyone in the house, and then—OMG, there they were, a long string of little silver bells, strung end-to-end across the porch, just like Jimmy's brother had said.

She looked and saw the old stone pathway, covered with moss and dead leaves. She didn't see any dead squirrel bones, or any other bones, for that matter. Maybe they'd all been cleared away? She looked at the bushes to the left of the path, spotting an area that looked just high enough for her to fit under. It'll be tight, she thought, but she could make it.

Stretched out on her belly, she pressed herself tight to the ground. She closed her eyes and started to crawl forward. Hearing the screen door open, she stopped and opened her eyes. She held her breath. Oh God, please no, she said to herself, don't eat me.

She heard an old woman's voice. "What are you doing on your belly like some poor fool? Stand up."

She didn't know what to do. She was too scared to move. Don't cry, she thought.

"Go on, get up. I won't boil and eat you, I've already had my supper."

She looked up at the old witch and looked away quickly, she might turn me to stone, she thought.

"Well? Get off the ground like some poor sick creature. Find your backbone, and just do it."

Alice pushed herself backwards, slowly, out from under the bushes. She started to stand, thinking, maybe she should run? And she did.

"Stop!"

Alice froze.

"You've a thorn caught on your coat, you might rip it." The old woman pointed. "See it there. Unhook it."

She looked at the old woman standing on the porch. She seemed ancient, small and frail and slightly bent forward. Gray hair in a bun at the back of her head. Otherwise, her clothes seemed kind of old person normal, no black dress or black cape or a pointy hat, nothing like that, just a summer dress with a pretty cardigan and black leather shoes with wide stubby heels.

She looked at her coat. She didn't want to touch the branch with the poisonous thorns.

"They're not poisonous, for goodness sake. It's just a rose bush."

She looked again at the thorn hooked into her coat. She reached for the branch, being careful not to touch the thorn.

She wanted to run again, but she looked at the silver bells. She wouldn't have one of those to show the others if she ran away.

"Is that what you've come for? One of my little silver bells?"

Alice nodded her head.

"You're the brave one amongst your group, I see. Come up here."

She didn't move.

"If you want one of my silver bells, you're going to have to trust me. The pathway is just a little overgrown, that's all. Push that branch forward, like a gate."

Alice looked back toward the road.

"If you're too frightened of an old rose bush, then go ahead and run away. But you won't get one of those," and she pointed to the string of silver bells hanging from the porch ceiling.

Alice tucked her hand into the sleeve of her coat and pushed the branch forward like a gate. She stepped forward.

"There now, look at that, you did it. Come up here and have a seat."

She walked up the porch stairs, looking above her at the string of silver bells.

"What's your name?"

"Alice."

"Have a seat, Alice, and we'll have ourselves a little chat, like proper neighbors. Would you like a glass of lemonade?"

With antifreeze, Alice thought. She heard herself saying, "Yes, please."

"Sit there and I'll be right back."

How was she gonna explain this? And what about Jimmy's brother? Those bushes weren't poisonous at all. And as far as she could tell, she wasn't even a witch. In fact, she seemed kind of nice and somewhat normal, for an old person living alone in the woods. "That lying—"

"Pardon me?"

"Oh, I'm sorry, ma'am."

"I should hope so. Here we go." She handed Alice a glass of lemonade and sat in the chair next to her. "It's good to see I'm still that old witch with poisonous bushes that killed her sister? I'd hate to think I'd lost my touch."

Alice looked at the woman. "You know about that?"

"Of course, I do. I've known about it for a long time. There were houses there before all of your new ones, you know. Not as many, of course, but enough, and there have been young boys and girls telling tall tales and seeking adventure for as long as I can remember."

"You mean it's not true?"

"It's Alice, right?"

"Yes."

"What's a witch, Alice? An old woman who lives on her own? Is that all it takes? No special powers? No flying brooms? If that's the case, the world is filled with witches. God willing, you'll be old yourself one day, and what will that make you? A witch, too? My sister was a dear sweet woman whom I loved very much. And I miss her to this day." She looked at the string of silver bells. "That's why I have those. I put one up each year on the anniversary of her death. Thirty-five, so far. And do you know why?"

Alice shook her head.

"Because when the wind blows, they chime, and it makes me think it's her, come back home for a visit, and that comforts me."

Alice looked at the bells.

"Would you like one?"

She looked at the woman and nodded.

"Well, then, we'll have to come to an understanding."

"An understanding?"

"Yes, you may have one of my little silver bells, to take back and show your friends, as your badge of courage—which, by the way, you were, very brave, and not only that, the first girl ever to make it here, and I'm so very proud of you for that. Yes, indeed, I am. It certainly took long enough. However, in exchange for one of my little silver bells, you will have to continue the myth of the witch in the woods."

"I will? Why?"

"You most certainly will. And why? Because it too has become a comfort to me. A mask I have come to enjoy wearing. Besides, I really don't want to be bothered by an endless stream of good-willed, or otherwise, people. And I look at it this way, I get to meet only the bravest of the brave. Not knowing when the next young one, like yourself, will show up, and it's always a welcome surprise. And then we have a visit, like you and I are now, and on their way they go. Until they come back, unknown to the others, and we have longer visits, getting to know one another better, watching them grow, their lives unfolding before me. And I have come to enjoy this very much."

"They come back?"

"Yes, of course they do. Not all, but many."

"Did Jimmy's brother come back?"

"Do you mean, Tommy? The tall skinny one that was her a few years ago?"

"Yes, Tommy Johnson."

"No. But perhaps he will yet."

"Can I come back?"

"Yes, of course you can, I would like that very much, as often as you like. But remember, you only just escaped with your life, having snuck under my poisonous bushes, evading my evil powers with your little silver bell clutched tightly in hand." She held out her closed hand. "Go on, hold your hand out."

Alice held her hand out and the woman placed a little silver bell there.

She looked at the bell.

"Go on then, you mustn't keep your friends waiting."

"Thank you."

"You're welcome, Alice. And don't forget our arrangement. You promise?"

"Yes, I promise. I won't forget."

"One more thing. When you look at that bell, do not think only of me, but of your bravery, and how in facing your fears, something good came of it—a lasting friendship."

"I will, thank you." And Alice walked down the stairs, stopping at the rose bush.

"Like a gate."

She looked back at the old woman making the motion of pulling back a gate.

She reached for the branch and took hold of it between the thorns and pulled it toward her, slipping through the opening. She turned and looked back at the woman. "Goodbye, and thank you. I'll be back for a visit."

"I know you will," and she watched Alice running through the woods, beneath the light of the moon, a little silver bell clutched tightly in her hand.

And just like that, the witch in the woods, snapped her fingers, and she was gone.

Love art and love life, they feed one another, and they will feed you. More art = a greater tolerance. A great tolerance = more life for everyone.

FOUR:
ART & LIFE

GOD, IF HE RESEMBLES ANYONE, IT'S TOM WAITS

As a writer of fiction, I am often asking questions—or questioning things, that have no answer. Of course, this is not exclusive to writers, far from it. And so, God. He shows up in my work. A lot, actually. Always in the same human form, and always dressed the same way. And he smokes. But then, of course, he does, why wouldn't he? It can't kill Him. It's my Bergman/strawberry thing.

The Fiddler in the Night: *He was sitting on a large white oak branch overhanging the river, wearing a purple vest, a green sports jacket, red pants, and a brown trilby hat tilted on an angle, his legs crossed, a cigarette burning down between his fingers, and he began to hum a hymn of hope to the rhythm of the current. I know you're out there, and I'll find you yet. I always do. He smoked more and he hummed more and he thought, true love, it's the only way forward, isn't that right, Fate, my darling?*

LOVE, GUNS & GOD in America: *He was rowing a small boat across the mouth of the Tidewater River, the sky* *a brilliant blue with no clouds, a light breeze, the shadows of big birds flying. My only point is this, it's become tedious. Tiresome, tedious, and predictable. These times of transition, they always make me anxious. Although, and he rowed more, putting his shoulders into it, it's one of my favorite parts of the things these people do. New gods with new stories and who the keeper of these stories will be? Soon, my lovely, not long now. Just the blink of an eye, really, one or two hundred more years. No time at all. My goodness, isn't it just all so wonderful? He put the oars up and let the boat drift. Lighting a cigarette, he leaned back and looked to the wide-open blue sky. He exhaled, and he began to hum again, all the world before him, and he thought, it'll be nice not to be God again, at least for a little while.*

I could go on, but it's clear to me now, God, if He resembles anyone, it's Tom Waits.

THE CAFÉ ORR

I'm drinking at the Café Orr in Montreal with Josip Novakovich, a master of short stories; of first person; of writing about his life. Camus comes to mind: "The absurd is the essential concept and the first truth." And this is Josip; this Josip writing. His ability to marry a sense of the improbability of life with ... 'well, of course, it happened.'

With the release of his latest book, *Vignettes*, we begin to talk about the 70s, his rock 'n' roll years, and me, just a kid viewing them in real time. They were the last free decade. That's what I think, and he says, he's not so sure about that. But then again, it's probably a common enough thought, when thinking about the years of one's childhood to associate this time in life with freedom. Or, was it simply the parents I had that installed in me this sense of freedom? My mother, a teacher and academic, who, although she cared for her kids, was occupied with other things. Her work, mostly. Fair enough. On a very normal day, my older brother, nine at the time, and myself, six, were at school, when our younger brother, just three, decided he wanted to know where we went each day and followed us. The principle called, "Nancy, how many kids do you have at school today?" She had no idea. And my father, Jake? Well, he was something else altogether, an old-time editor: Irish whiskey, cigars, and a blue grease pencil. His thoughts of our well-being ran in the direction of, "When the streets lights come on it's time to get home." Later, in our early teen years, you were either home in time or locked out of the house, and I can't tell you how many nights I spent sleeping in the car. It seemed normal, and I was appreciative of the possibility of it. Much like I was the first, of the many times, he gave me the strap. He would say, "Don't move, I don't want hit your kidneys." And I remember thinking: What the fuck is a kidney? I didn't know, but I did know, if Jake told me it was not a good thing for him to hit them—with his folded leather belt, I knew better than to move.

As kids in the 70s we had hippies as elementary school teachers that were clearly stoned, and to my memory, stoned well, while listening to The Rolling Stones at the back of the classroom with headphones. Is it surprising, then, our generation immediately following the hippies, a generation as young kids that watched everything turn chemical, had instilled in us a spirit of 'anything goes?' The adults in the room basically having had the keys to the future taken from them by the now fading-out, becoming jaded, hippies. Happy enough, I suppose, this older generation, of committing to jumping into this new pool of disposable everything to make some money. Of course, by then, for many, the drugs themselves had become the thing, the limits being pushed beyond any previous known boundaries—Hello, 27 Club, and to this day, I do think that if you can make it to 28, you'll be okay. It was really quite something, open classrooms, stoned teachers, acid rain, the mass arrival of plastic, and fast food, without the knowledge yet, or means, of managing any of it. It was wild, and it was unruly, and it was a hot mess, this imperfect blooming of a disposable society.

It was freedom, until it wasn't, which, of course, gave us the 80s—the let's tame it all down and just look—IDK, anything but real, because, honestly, who wants to die at 27? Or, to have to think about protecting your kidneys?

And yet, I miss the unpredictability of that time, the wide-openness of no one really knowing what the fuck they were doing, or why, or that, being uninformed as a society to that degree gave birth to an absurdity that was the first, if not possibly, the only truth, from which, I'm convinced, a certain greatness was incubated that became the tech. boom, should you have been fortunate enough to make it past 27, with your kidneys intact.

And Josip, he looks at me, and he says, IDK, I just wanted to play some rock 'n' roll.

MORE MCCARTHY

We recently said goodbye to the American writer Cormac McCarthy, July 20, 1933 - June 13, 2023. A writer who did not receive a single royalty check from one of his first four books over a period of twenty-eight years. And yet, he kept on. Why? Did he know he was a writer future students of American literature would look at a map and draw a line connecting the names, Twain, Melville, Faulkner – McCarthy? Perhaps. But he never lost sight of what he did have: His faith and his hope, his trust in himself.

All art is storytelling, and there is just one story: I was here. If and when the world wants your art, it'll find it. Go and ask Melville. And now, too, go and ask McCarthy.

A new McCarthy novel, *The Passenger*, and what to make of it? "If we are not after essence, Squire, then what are we after? And I'll defer to your view that we cannot uncover such a thing without putting our stamp upon it." Which is what McCarthy did with this book. Both things:

Reaching to essence, while putting his stamp as a writer upon that searching.

Told from each of their perspectives, Bobby Western mourns the death (suicide) of his younger, schizophrenic sister, Alicia Western, while being pursued by the US government for a crime—possibly, that remains unknown, to us, if not, to him. Shadowing both of them is their father's past as one of the architects of the atomic bomb.

As always, a McCarthy novel is a joyful ride with words, and here, too, this is true. It is not in the storytelling that this book is a departure from his previous work, it is in the goals of the story itself, as if the story was in no need of its own form: The randomness of life lived within the realm of the unknown while studying its own refection of its own telling as the precision of mathematics and physics look on, unable to offer any relief. But then, a story of grief and loss is always a tragedy, for what we feel a loss for, we are less, it becoming our reality—the lessor of us. Which is this book, the acknowledgment of this. A book without a linear need—no cause and effect here. A book uncaring of the outcome, which is what? Quite simply, it is McCarthy saying, I am a writer, and after a life lived as a writer—asking questions to which there are no answers, I still have no answers, and therefore, I am in no need of a form within which to put the pretext of an answer, or the need of a form building to an answer, and I shall not try. Consider: It is a book centered around a missing passenger that is never found. A relationship between a brother and sister that is never defined. A crime that is never named. Questions without answers, the main one being: Are our pasts any more real than the products of a schizophrenic mind? Is the passenger, that's drowned and never found, a version of ourselves we carry forward? If so, drown them, and let them never be found. Free yourself. Which is what it seems McCarthy has done with this book, to have freed himself as a writer—giving himself permission to reach to more, while being less, and becoming even more in the process. And it reads as if he knew this is what he was writing, and why, and most importantly, when. And I like that, and I tip my hat to him, for having the courage to go out that way.

McCarthy was often criticized for being a writer of male fiction. Or, his inability to write women well. True enough, and something he acknowledged himself. And so, it was with great joy, while reading this book, discovering the wonderfully formed, transgender character, Debussy Fields. A shot at all those who choose to make ignorance and fear their companion. "He watched her until she was lost among the tourists. Men and women alike turning to look after her. He thought that God's goodness appeared in strange places. Dont close your eyes."

As for *The Passenger's* companion piece, *Stella Maris,* I liked the idea of this, the breaking out of a character's insights, not only with respect to filling in *The Passenger's* narrative, but for its own sake—more of who she was, and why. And much like *The Passenger,* McCarthy gets to freewheel into a world that interests him—thoughts he had wanted to share, again, without the concern of normal narrative structures, or the feeling of having to wrap things up, with answers, to anything—a total sense of freedom. I'll just write. I'll please myself. And why shouldn't he have, after a lifetime of writing? Oh, and then there's this, which is quite something, his last published words:

"I think our time is up.

I know. Hold my hand.

Hold your hand?

Yes. I want you to.

All right. Why?

Because that's what people do when they're waiting for the end of something."

Thanks for the body of work, Cormac McCarthy.

He was here.

And there shall be now no more words

falling from his pen.

WHAT I KNOW ABOUT WRITING

Bob Dylan, speaking to an interviewer, said, "The best songs I ever wrote are the songs I knew nothin' about." Leo Tolstoy, walking by, he heard this, and he said, "All we can know is that we know nothing." Toni Morrison, on her way to class, said, "But what of chaos, confusion, disorder?" "That's it," said Hunter, looking over the top of his aviator sunglasses, a lit cigarette burning down in its holder in his mouth. "Buy the ticket, take the ride." At which point Elvis left the building and Tom Waits climbed up through a buttonhole. Albert Einstein, out for a walk, saw them all, and he said, "It's true, imagination is everything." It was then, that very fine gentleman, Mr. Keats, standing next to a stranger waiting on a bus, said, "I am certain of nothing but of the holiness of the heart's affections and the truth of the imagination." And William Faulkner, he thought for a moment, and he said, "I am nothing more than a wet seed wild in the hot blind earth, and that's good enough for me." James Joyce, well, he heard it all, and he laughed, and he said, "WTF?"

He finished his glass of white wine and walked out the pub door and putting his hand to the blinding sun, said, "Write dangerously." And me? I looked at Joyce, in that other place and time, and before I could say, "That's a good idea," Émile Nelligan, with crumbs of food in his beard, fell out of his chair, laughing - mad as a hatter, and he said, "What is left of us in this brief storm?"

Good question.

And Sheila Watson, in her remembering, whispered, "Émile, it's okay, for it is true, the word is a flame burning in a dark glass."

And that's it: What I know about writing.

... oh, and this, of course: The joy in reaching to the truth in writing is having the faith to trust that it can be found, provided one looks to the pulse of blood running through the veins of thought, and not to the meaning of it.

THE LITTLE BOOK YOU HAVEN'T READ, BUT SHOULD

A good book must be more than just a collection of symbols and meanings, it must hold us and take us with it, taking care in its knowing of us; our conditions; our dreams; our fears. It must enlighten us, allowing for the progression of our greatest possibilities.

And that is exactly what *The Double Hook* does.

Media guru Marshal McLuhan and Yale professor and formalist critic Cleanth Brooks both considered it a "literary landmark."

Jack McClelland said, "It made money for McClelland and Stewart. If it didn't, we would still consider it one of the best books that it has been our privilege to publish."

And yet? Today? Nothing. Why? Because Sheila was a woman writing in Canada in the 1950s?

From 1934 to 1936 Sheila Watson taught nine grades in a one-room schoolhouse in Dog Creek, British

Columbia, Canada, on the banks of the Fraser River, in the Cariboo district. A place and time that forms the setting of *The Double Hook.*

"I sank roots," Watson said, "that I have never been able to disentangle."

She wrote the book between 1952 and 1954 in Calgary, Alberta and revised it in Paris from 1956 to 1957.

Watson, "It's about how people are driven, how if they have no art, how if they have no tradition, how if they have no ritual, they are driven in one of two ways, either towards violence or towards insensibility - if they have no mediating rituals which manifest themselves in what I suppose we call art forms." Violence, or insensibility. The reasons why, according to Watson, we need our art forms, and our traditions. `

The setting is an unnamed community of only a dozen individuals, divided and isolated by their fears and loneliness, their uncertainties, lost and clinging to the parched banks of a winding river run dry in a hot July drought. A place forgone of its own past and outside connections. Barren of all traditions and rituals.

And so they search, for these rituals, these traditions, for meaningful connections, between themselves, and others. "I've seen Ma standing with the lamp by the fence, she said. Holding it up in broad daylight. I've seen her standing looking for something even the birds couldn't see. Something hid from every living thing. I've seen her defying. I've seen her take her hat off in the sun at noon, baring her head and asking for the sun to strike her. Holding the lamp and looking where there's nothing to be found. Nothing but dust."

This is reminiscent of Greek philosopher, Diogenes of Sinope, founder of Cynicism, with his lamp held high in daylight looking for one good man. It was also Diogenes, who upon looking over a pile of human bones, was said to have said to Alexander the Great, "I am searching for the bones of your father but cannot distinguish them from those of a slave." A statement also relevant to us, for as Watson says in the book, "One man's one man and two men or ten men aren't something else."

Margret Atwood, writing about *The Double Hook* in *Survival: A Thematic Guide to Canadian Literature*, says, "While alive the old lady's sin had been her refusal to accept life whole, the 'darkness' along with the 'light', the cyclical processes of Nature as well as man's structures, houses, and straight lines. The 'something she'd never found' is her own completeness."

In Watson's narrative, she looks beyond morality tales of Christian redemption and Greek philosophy, reaching back to Native American mythology. "I don't know about God, William said. Your god sounds only a step from the Indian's coyotes." And then again here, the coyote calling: "In my mouth is forgetting. In my darkness is rest."

In a February 1975 interview with the Capilano Review, Watson said, "When I began the work which became *The Double Hook*, I knew I had to create a total fiction out of experience which was concrete—which defied the clichés imposed on it. I wanted to get rid of reportage, the condescension of omniscience. It wasn't an act of reconstruction—like going back and saying I remember this—no one I ever knew did or said the things which are done and said." She continued, "I wanted to fuse the dialogue with the context—the reaching towards speech—the speaking out of silence—out of space."

Sheila Watson's, *The Double Hook*, is a near flawless transcending of the historical boundaries of language and the societal conventions of narrative style. Watson marries form and structure with essence—i.e., the intention and inspiration of 'self'; our intuitive thinking—using emotive imagery to drive the words.

And so, why then, has this book not broken out of the confinements of academia and literary studies? Was it because Watson was a woman writing in the 1950s in British Columbia? Or was it because the book was labeled 'modernist,' an expression of narrative that lived outside of the accepted commercial standards and forms of that time?

I don't know. I do know, however, that the book today is still considered a work of modernist writing. And what does that say about us? About writing today? And so, yes, I think we should be holding it up, saying—this is still possible. Find it. Find this and push harder.

Certainly, it is not too late to come back to the work. Look at Melville and *Moby Dick*, a perfect example of time (sixty-six years) before we caught up to it, and once we had, what that did for writing.

Read *The Double Hook*. A book that, although written sixty-five years ago, still reads today, as if it were written tomorrow.

In the long winding days of my life, in the solitary moments of each pre-day's dark, I remember:

FIVE:
LOVE AGAIN

ANOTHER BEAUTIFUL STORMY DAY TOMORROW

There's a big moon up there,
Over these days now.
You've got my Neil Young shirt.
My jean jacket.

On the road, barefoot and shades, the music on the radio bouncing off country neon.

There'll be money falling from the pages of these books one day, with words there to see, and will it be art? Or, art then? Who knows? Godot, you and me, that's who.

And now, in these days still; this imperfect bliss of us, like a bag of cocaine, a broken crow's nest—in the wind, barefoot and shades, the music on the radio bouncing off Montreal graffiti walls.

And will it be enough, yet? Will it ever be?

Who knows? Godot, you and me, that's who, all these words still falling on these pages still.

And in these days now one day, another beautiful stormy day tomorrow, we'll listen to a night with no sounds coming, in the woods, by the lake, under that one big moon, our shadows stretched long on the road before us.

And I'll say,

Baby, it feels like rain.

EIGHT DAYS IN JULY

He doesn't really know what is waiting—yes, he does, he thinks, and he's tried to touch that and hold it, and yet, there are still these questions of coming back into the folds of life, each mile a known unknowing on the highways of hoping with eyes watching, the distilled—not broken, certainly, needing eyes, one more mile driven without easy answers falling from the sky that day, play the radio, the music louder, another mile on the road away from the waiting times. Which is what? Don't look away. Born of what? He doesn't. And now another mile on that road to you.

You'd written your first book and I'd read it and liked it and wrote a review, even though I wasn't fully sure what to make of it, not the writing, that was there and waiting more, but the story—although, who's to say, not me and not you, and we'll go and ask the gods about that, one day. The words on the page reaching to essence, there just below the words. It didn't matter—well okay then, tell me who you are? And yes, I see you like the Habs, and you're a writer, and you have two kids, but tell me more, tell me not your pages—your page, I'll take your words on a line; the spoken words of us, and it took five weeks, the six-thirty of our time.

He had a plan his one son called a plan that wasn't a plan, but then, whoever knows what is out there and waiting, in this world of what is real and what is imagined (which will become more in different ways and he won't know this). "What you seek is seeking you." Is that true? Either way, it's a hell of a thought, isn't it? Just like, "the road is walking too," which just might mean, there is what you see and there is what you want to see, or what you've been told to see. But either way, he had a car and he knew he'd be on the move, and hopefully, it wouldn't be on that road walking too, at least, not too much, not this time, or if it was, it would be in the ways of the here and now that were good and true and solid under foot. He would hope for that, just like he'd hope there'd be endless amounts of gas in the tank to keep on moving—to keep seeking, in the land of lakes and rivers, a land of magic made of granite, on a canoe with not much more. Something to write with. Is that not a plan? After all the years of chaos not solved that always felt like never being enough, he wanted a simple quiet, a quiet made of moving over still water between large outcroppings of shield rock streaked with black and pink and where alder bushes, raspberry bushes, and trees grew from crevices, and where ancient trees grown too tall and heavy for their rocky moorings had fallen onto their sides, their great circular walls of exposed roots and dirt pointing to the light of vacant skies under which there would also be endless rows of sun-seeking trees still growing.

In the mornings I'd find you, this you I was coming to know, and it would settle over me, in such meaningful and powerful and pulling—real ways, and I knew this because of the words I was sending to you. The well of these words a place I knew—still, apparently, and trusted, not that, 'how is this possible?' was not there in the room with me like some bat-shit crazy woman with tobacco and tattoos—vengeance on her mind, screaming: You are not that person! Not anymore! Move on! Look away! You have a plan. And yet, with each passing day I did not look away, and neither did you, and there would be the next day's six-thirty coming; the next day's walking in gratitude, hearing the words: "I walk in my truth." Words I hear still; words I heard for the first time standing on a stump in a field looking around for the resounding of them—which happened, they did come back, over and over, they came back to me.

When the cold to stay would blow in, he would have left the water, the granite, the healing magic of the quiet, turning to running with the sun, wanting nothing more than the slow, easy warming of it upon him. It wouldn't have mattered how long he'd have stayed in one place, how long in another place, just the sun, and the quiet evenings for writing and whispering to his kids in the dark, I hope you're well? I miss you. He'd look down, perhaps, at the words he'd written, words that might have said: Do not let your fear be the thing that brings about your fear happening. And that, too, he would think, is a blueprint.

In a picture I saw you were leaning over a desk and it was your eyes in the time of a plague that held me. And were they eyes that were practised eyes? Broken eyes? Eyes that were saying ... what? But it was just a picture—one word, a thousand and one words, move on. But I didn't, I looked more, and kept looking, and then in the six-thirties of our time, looking yet, the miles now almost behind me, here—driving into Quebec, not lost, but off the map, and I'm late. I pulled off the road into the parking lot of a baseball field and parked under a big tree. There was a dépanneur across the road and I went there and bought a bottle of water. I walked back to the car, drinking the water, and I changed my shirt—it had been a long drive, seven hours, so far. Standing in the shade of that big tree, drinking the water, I began to think, is this happening? Can it be? This running to you? Can five weeks talking on the telephone do this? I'd just left my four kids at home for eight days in July. I smiled, and thought, yes it can be, when one does not look away. All the miles almost done now.

All the miles all done, getting out of the car, seeing you for the first time. A long narrow summer dress to your ankles, your bare shoulders, and those eyes, eyes that I realized then, were never eyes before that moment, saying: hold me; hold us, keep the six-thirty of us here, alive, and always wanting more. It had been a question in our minds, what would happen in that moment, who would move first, and then what? It wasn't me, it was you, my meeting you in a moment frozen in time still—a moment that understood immediately the meaning of us. And I can see you still, turning, lifting your dress, walking up the stairs to the door of that small cabin on the lake, looking back at me, and smiling, with eyes now that said, yes to the six-thirty of all our time.

And for eight days in July, we made that true, and are still, for we shall not let our fear be the thing that brings about our fear happening, will we? And you say, we can be the warm rain and moonlit breezes and quiet silences we deserve, the warming sun upon us. And I say, with no need of solace, for there is no need of it, in the eight days in July of our life, the six-thirty of all our time, as we continue to walk in our truth, with gratitude.

And do you remember? These days, the days before the eight days in July:

May 22, 2021, 8:00 AM

NG: Good morning Christian. First, thanks for the generous review. :) I bought your book. I just broke my leg and have not been sleeping well, and it's difficult to concentrate, but I think I'm in for a treat... Leaving for cottage in ten days. That's where reading will happen. And yes, Leafs will most likely win. Still, we've all become real Catholics here in Montreal. We believe... Man we are nuts. Take care.

May 23, 2021, 10:00 AM

CF: Thank you for your message, it's very kind of you. As for my review - I really liked your book, and it was a pleasure to write it. You write well. I kept it short, in an attempt to reach potential readers. I'm sorry to hear you broke your leg. I hope it's not too bad and it heals well. Thanks for buying my book - I would have been pleased to send you one. The novel? Or the collection of stories?

May 23, 2021, 11:28 AM

NG: The Fiddler in the Night is what I bought. Hope your day is going great. Bonne journée :)

May 27, 2021, 10:17 AM

CF: It's a beautiful day - I hope your leg is feeling okay?

May 27, 2021, 11:04 AM

NG: Pain is manageable. Seeing orthopedist tomorrow.

May 27, 2021, 11:11 AM

CF: Have you been able to write, or has it been too distracting in discomfort type ways, with your leg?

May 27, 2021, 11:21 AM

NG: Not much since leg broke. Just a little. This year has been challenging space-wise. My two kids have landed with me... Writing has suffered, I rarely have time to get into a zone. Not complaining. We have a good time. I read, do lots of research. I lost my office to ████. That's why I rented a cottage for two months. To write more. Hopefully better too. I need to put off surgery to after July. Normal is just around the corner. Then everyone will get back to their lives. In their own apartment... But fun and funny moments happened. For that I'm grateful.

May 27, 2021, 11:39 AM

CF: Yes ... I am as well (grateful). Sept for me, after what seems like a very long time ... I mean, beyond just COVID ...

May 28, 2021, 7:50 AM

CF: How did it go? Everything okay?

May 28, 2021, 7:59 AM

NG: I think so. I needed an MRI, but couldn't get appointment beforehand. Dr. is upset and will push for MRI ASAP. There is a piece of bone floating. We need to know how far from its original spot it is. Arthroscopic surgery would fix that. Then the ligament tears. ACL, PCL? Again MRI will tell if I need ligament reconstruction. I read your story, Christian (A Look Back and Say Goodbye) ... Je suis désolée ... I feel the pain and the love and the hopelessness. How powerless we feel when faced with it.

May 28, 2021, 8:06 AM

CF: I hope you get the MRI soon, so you can get these things resolved. How's the pain? It sounds like you did a real number on it. I hope you have people helping to take care of you? Thanks for reading... things just went on for too long, and I took a bit of a hit, but working my way back from that. I guess, that's mostly what the story is about. That, and just trying to understand. It'll be nice to get the kids back on their own individual paths, I'm looking forward to it – for them, I'll miss them, however, terribly. In the meantime, just trying to get this third book done. It's absolutely pouring rain here ...

May 28, 2021, 8:09 AM

NG: Hum. Friends are taking care of me. Kids, coffee in the morning is what I get ... :)

May 28, 2021, 6:21 PM

NG: I started your book.

May 28, 2021, 6:22 PM

CF: Thanks. I hope you like it.

May 28, 2021, 6:22 PM

NG: I do. Your words. I can easily see how they would compel an audience during a reading. Mine. Not so much. Writing came later for me.

May 28, 2021, 6:49 PM

CF: I got away from it for a very long time. Too long.

May 28, 2021, 7:52 PM

CF: From 2010 until 2012, we were just trying to figure everything out, you know, with what happened, [redacted] and that's when I moved us up to the cottage ... 4 kids [redacted] in a cabin on a lake in the middle of nowhere so I could write, and it's when I really started to go at it, and it was a nightmare ... but it wasn't, too.

May 28, 2021, 7:53 PM

NG: So many of us pushback without reason, or curiosity when confronted.

May 28, 2021, 7:56 PM

NG: It would be a waste if we resisted all the time for too long.

May 28, 2021, 7:57 PM

NG: I guess you never wanted to write about it directly, share ur story.

May 28, 2021, 7:58 PM

CF: It's hard to explain, except to say, there were no answers, and so... it's like, not knowing vs knowing, and I guess that's what I was setting out to explore, the not knowing. expectations, too.

May 28, 2021, 7:58 PM

CF: fiction was my way of doing that.

May 28, 2021, 7:59 PM

NG: I understand that :)

May 28, 2021, 8:02 PM

NG: There is space in your writing.

May 28, 2021, 8:02 PM

C: The book is a bit different, in structure, I guess.

May 29, 2021, 5:26 AM

CF: Hope the coffee is good ...

May 29, 2021, 5:26 AM

NG: Sleep was okay. Coffee was perfect. :)

May 29, 2021, 5:37 AM

CF: Maybe you were worrying about the Habs in your sleep? I really enjoyed our conv. last night, and so, thanks again.

May 29, 2021, 5:46 AM

NG: I did too...

May 29, 2021, 5:46 AM

CF: Mtl is lucky to have you ... and if they were smart, they'd win for you.

May 29, 2021, 5:47 AM

NG: That's almost romantic... :)

May 29, 2021, 5:47 AM

CF: Well ... yes, I guess it is. :)

May 29, 2021, 9:17 AM

NG: On my way to coffee, the homeless woman who chose my neighborhood as her home was posted in a different spot. I've been walking by her for 4 years. She is different, feels different. I had ~~truies été~~ eye contact with her before but most of the time she was gone. Today I finally spoke with her and got her what she craved ... fruits, a muffin, and a coffee. One cream one sugar. I introduced myself and she told me her name too. Lucie. Finally.

May 29, 2021, 9:18 AM

CF: That's nice that you did that.

May 29, 2021, 9:19 AM

NG: There were no reasons not to.

May 29, 2021, 9:21 AM

CF: But do not think for a min., that's brought good karma to your Habs :)

May 29, 2021, 9:21 AM

NG: Lol

May 29, 2021, 3:19 PM

CF: Good luck tonight. I know you're watching the game with your dad, so I shall save all condolences for the end. Hope you remembered the beer ... & tissues. GLG

May 29, 2021, 7:08 PM

NG: You sent me condolences...!

May 29, 2021, 7:08 PM

CF: well ... yeah

May 30, 2021, 3:39 AM

NG: Can't sleep. Looking forward to those mornings at cottage.

May 30, 2021, 3:40 AM

NG: The lake. The quiet. The bears!

May 30, 2021, 3:40 AM

CF: Those damn bears.

May 30, 2021, 3:41 AM

CF: ... so glad you're doing that.

May 30, 2021, 3:45 AM

NG: Who cooks in your house?

May 30, 2021, 3:47 AM

CF: A number of years ago it was best for everyone involved that they start cooking for themselves. Mostly it happened that way bc ███ went Vegan - █████ vegetarian. 4 yrs. ago, maybe.

May 30, 2021, 4:38 AM

NG: I'm half way through your book - and yes I do, I like it! BUT. I obviously spot one word easily in all the books I read. I usually don't see it that often. Do you know how many times you wrote... Inhaled?

May 30, 2021, 4:38 AM

CF: No - I'm not even aware I wrote it - in Fiddler?

May 30, 2021, 4:38 AM

NG: Yes.

May 30, 2021, 4:39 AM

CF: I'm trying to think where ... oh, I know.

May 30, 2021, 4:39 AM

CF: ... with smoking. I have a thing for making god smoke. My Bergman/strawberry thing.

May 30, 2021, 5:08 AM

NG: Chris... finish your book... then a proper meet?

May 30, 2021, 5:09 AM

CF: Nathalie, yes. I'd like that.

And that's how it happened, in the time of a plague, when two writers met, one from Toronto, one from Montreal.

"They did not know it was impossible so they did it"
— Mark Twain

---

*Culled from 146,865 words of text messaging, May 22, 2021 – July 6, 2021.

* The HABS *somehow* won the series, and the Leafs/HABS rivalry continues, the words, too.

*The book was *LOVE, GUNS & GOD in America*, and it was finished in Montreal.

A LETTER TO MY CHILDREN

When I'm gone, come sit with me, next to this garden, the sun warming upon your face, and remember, and in this remembering, smile, through tears or not, for I will be there with you—how could it not be so? Our joy; our love, and such happiness, it was ours, and will be still, in that place just beyond these words; that garden, where I shall know always the limitlessness of our days, and what they meant to me, a light my passing can do nothing to dim.

HOPE LASTING

The young girl woke and she opened her eyes. It was quiet.

It was still.

Everything so perfectly quiet and perfectly still, and was she dreaming? Did it matter? The forest air holding a scent of some deep wanting of some previous unknowingness. That's what she thought. And where was she? This place?

She sat up, covered in leaves. She looked at the forest, magical in its holding of her, but she did not know this yet. She looked to the trees, majestic in their reaching, the crowns just within her sight, the sun there, breaking through to her, and she felt, somehow, as if she was standing beneath a canopy of new life; new days, days that just might hold the possibility of hope lasting, like a wish made somewhere, by someone, sometime.

Brushing the leaves away, she stopped—there was a small heart-shaped golden locket with a thin gold chain wrapped around her left hand. She brought it to her and she touched it, the smoothness of it. She saw a latch and she pressed it. It wouldn't open. She looked around her, and she wondered again, where was she?

She touched herself, to see if she was real—and she thought, she felt real. She brushed more of the leaves away, and she stood. She touched her hair, as if measuring the length of it. She looked again at the locket and she untangled it from her hand, watching it twirl in the light, and she asked to the trees; to the light; to the ground holding below her, where'd it come from, and why do I have it?

She began to walk among the endless rows of towering trees, and she told herself, I'm not frightened, walking in a forest all alone, even though she did not know who she was, what her name was, or why she was there. And yet, it felt to her as if all of that was okay—that she would be okay. And yet, she thought, it would be nice to know who I am. At least, just a little bit.

A boy, fully formed in his boy-ness, and not partially formed, woke. He, too, was covered in dry, colorful leaves. And like the girl, he did not know where he was. Who he was. And there, wrapped in his left hand, was the same golden locket. Next to him was a wolf, its coat of fur reflecting back the tree light. Sensing the boy stirring beneath the pile of leaves, the wolf opened its eyes.

Walking, the young girl was happy, and she stopped, before her was a wall of mist. She reached her finger to it. Could she touch it? Would it burn her? Her finger falling off and dropping to the ground? The quiet in the stillness of that place, settling upon her, and she knew then, it would be okay. She closed her eyes and moved her finger forward. She opened her eyes, her hand was gone, but she could feel herself wiggling her fingers on the other side of the mist. She brought her hand back, and she walked into the mist.

What's your name?

But, of course, the wolf did not answer. It looked around, and it looked back at the small boy, who almost spoke out loud the word, yes, when the thought appeared in his mind that they should start walking. And as they did, he put his hand to the top of the wolf's head, scratching behind its ear, the good feel of its warm fur.

In the mist, the young girl walked slower, careful of her footing.

What was that?

She looked around, and there before her, she saw countless numbers of small young children, just like her, dressed in thin and ragged clothing. Appearing. Disappearing. And now adults, of all kinds. Some holding in their arms, still and quiet babies. It saddened her, but she was not frightened, and she continued to walk.

Animals now, too, were moving in and out of the mist.

Wolves, she thought.

More children.

More adults, with babies held in their arms, that did not make a sound.

She walked out from the mist and found herself standing in an endless valley meadow. The sun there, hard upon the tall grass.

Standing next to her, as if waiting for her, was a wolf, identical to the one with the boy.

The young girl said, hi, what's your name? I don't know mine, otherwise, I would tell you. And she said, yes, we should keep walking. And like the boy, she put her hand to the top of the wolf's head, the good feel of its warm fur.

In the middle of the valley field, she saw an old oak tree. She looked more, there was something beneath the shade of the tree, but it was too far and she could not tell what it was.

She walked toward the old oak tree, in the tall, warm grass, her hand coming to it.

Beneath the tree there was a caravan-type trailer, the trim painted in bright colors, the grass up past the door, the wheels taken by the earth. On the side boards of the trailer, in faded painted letters, was the word, Circus.

Sitting on the hitch of the trailer was an old man with beautiful olive skin, a straw, sweat-stained trilby hat, purple pants, black pointy shoes, a white shirt, a green vest. His legs were crossed, a cigarette burning down between his fingers. Hello, Issy.

My name's Issy?

It's a nice enough name, don't you think?

Yes, I do. I like it. She looked around. Where am I? This place?

Well, it's here, of course, and he stood, looking around at the day, as if taking pride in it. It is a beautiful day, though, is it not?

Yes, said Izzy, it is, and I don't really ever remember a day quite like it.

No?

No, not really.

Well, Izzy, I think so, too.

Izzy smiled.

I suppose, said the old man, I should get going, I can't be sitting around here talking and doing nothing on a beautiful day such as this, there's work to be done yet.

There is? said Izzy, and she felt a sense of loss, just for a moment, as if this only other person she'd met was special to her. Wanting him to stay with her longer.

I think, if I were you, I'd walk that way, and he pointed.

Izzy looked to where he pointed, and she pointed, too. That way?

Yes.

A small breeze picked up and Izzy tilted her head back, hearing a voice somewhere inside of it, saying, yes, this way.

The old man tipped his hat, it's been nice meeting you, Izzy, and I hope we meet again, one day. I'm sure we will.

She looked at the old man. It was nice meet you, too, she said, and she thanked him.

You're welcome. And don't worry, Izzy, you'll be fine. Isidore will see to it.

Isidore?

Yes, he's waiting for you.

He is?

Yes. Well, good luck, Izzy, and he opened the trailer door and walked inside.

She walked the large valley meadow, and after what seemed like a very long time, she came to another forest. The shade of the trees felt good, it was cool, and it was quiet, and she thought, which way now? She looked at the wolf, and she said, what do you think? The wolf turned away and looked at a big black bird sitting on the branch of a tree, and the bird said, do you not see the direction the tree is pointing? And sure enough, the entire tree was formed in the shape of an arrowhead, pointing the way. It's a moon tree, said the bird, and the bird flew away.

Thank you, bird, said Izzy, and they started on their way.

The young boy, having come to the same valley meadow as Izzy, in a different part of it, had come across the same old man, the same old trailer. Had had the same conversation. And now, he, too, with the wolf next to him, walked in the new forest, and after a very long time, they came upon the same talking black bird, which showed them the way.

The edge of the forest was in sight, and there, in that place, Izzy saw a light, of its own, or so it seemed to her. Standing in the intensity of the light was a very large man, his back to her. She walked from the forest, and as she did, she looked to her left, where she saw the young boy and his wolf exiting the forest at the very same time as she and her wolf did.

Walking their own paths, they met at the man, each of them standing on their side of him, who did not look down at either one, but instead, continued to look at that which was before him.

The children looked, at the black and scorched earth. The slow swirling grey ash of what once was.

The man looked at Izzy. You're here?

Yes, said Izzy. Are you Isidore?

I am, he said, and he looked at the young boy. You're Finn?

Yes, said the boy.

Good, said Isidore. Shall we go?

Where? said the boy.

Home, of course, and he took their hands and turned and walked away from that old dead world now, the grey ash of yesterday still falling.

Izzy, feeling the golden locket against her chest, put her hand to it.

Next to her, so, too, did Finn. He stopped and he looked at Izzy. What do you think is inside?

Izzy stopped and looked at Finn. I don't know.

Isidore stopped.

Both wolves stopped.

Izzy, smiling, said, maybe one day, we'll find out.

Finn, looking at Izzy, realized, for the very first time, he was lost to the depth of purity in her beautiful green eyes, and he said, yes, I think we will.

Good, she said, and they took the man's hands again and continued to walk, the golden lockets against their chests, shining in the light of everyone's new day.

THE EARLY POEMS, PART TWO

The Voice of Yesterday

The soul of the people,
Is the voice of yesterday,
A voice that is,
Most assuredly,
The sound of old hearts crying,
In the night.
Long ago, it's what I wrote,
On a piece of paper.
And to that boy, I say:
They cry still.
And so, that's it I guess,
Then and now,
What I know
About the human race.

To see, and to hold us, is love. And what possibly could be wrong ... with a little more simplicity in our patience? Compassion in our understanding? Remembering gratitude? Because, well, fate might just be listening, and if so, coaxing time to work for us—not against us, in these days of our humanity, not yet seen.

POSTSCRIPT: HUMANITY

WHY WON'T AMERICA FIX ITSELF?

Yes, the question is rhetorical, the hope of America actually doing this, that thought having left the building of reasonable expectations some time ago. But the why holds up, at least from a speculation point of view. It's not as if the issues that plague and hold America back aren't well known.

And even more frustrating, that the answers to these issues are also widely known. There are any number of countries, right now, that are progressing in healthy, free market, democratic ways, devoid of high rates of poverty, economic policies fueling unhealthy levels of income inequality that strangle the flow of capital, healthcare systems that work—and help, without bankrupting people, education systems, meant to do just that—to educate, publicly, equally. And then, of course, there's the social side of things, politicians trying to legislate morality. The promotion of 'family values,' the kind that prevents your straight white child from walking into a public washroom and coming upon a she/her trans person and having their fresh young DNA altered in unimaginable ways, forever. What books are appropriate to read, which aren't. The bible—not science. Abortion, a greater issue beyond who you are. Etc.

"The liberty of a democracy is not safe if the people tolerate the growth of private power to a point where it becomes stronger than their democratic state itself. That, in its essence, is fascism—ownership of government by an individual, by a group, or by any other controlling private power." Franklin D. Roosevelt, April 29, 1938. And that's as good a definition of fascism as any, and important to understand, when viewing America today.

When a former President (Jimmy Carter) publicly states this (September 2017), you have to figure the cat is pretty much all the way out of the bag: "I would say that we've become kind of more of an oligarchy than we have a democracy, now. The rich people and the powerful people in our country decide a lot of who gets the nomination and therefore who is elected to office—not just presidents but senators and governors and Congress members." And that was in 2017. And it just keeps getting worse, not better. Not yet.

Without the working principal of the 'will of the people,' there can be no working democracy. There can be no American Dream. For what is the American Dream, if not the will of the people operating within the framework of a system that creates and promotes social mobility. And today, in America, social mobility is dead.

Back to the question, why won't America fix itself? In what other field of enterprise, be it medicine, accounting, law, business, does accountability not matter? Since 1980, where the road starts that has led us to where we are today, there have only been two parties in power. Two parties responsible for the current state of affairs. And we'll stop right there, and say this: save the red/blue finger pointing, it's tired, and it's boring. Not to mention, not accurate. And that is part of the answer, too, of why won't America fix itself. There has been no reversal of public policy that would have, at the very least, delayed, if not deterred America from this march toward fascism. For fascism is nothing more than an ultimate form of self-interest. It is, the entitlement of the entitled, protected and perpetuated. And like moths to the glass of a light at night that cuts to the bone, each day, more and more, in too many places, for too long, populism grows from under this: The asking of the right questions, and reaching, over and over again, to the wrong answers. Greed and perpetuated self-interest nurturing neglect that equals pain and suffering for more and more people, each day. It can't hold. It won't hold.

In 1980, America was the leading lender of money to other countries, with a debt-to-GDP ratio of 31 percent. Today, America borrows more money than any other country, and has a debt-to-GDP ratio of 127.5 percent. This is called, being upside down. It's called, failure. And yet … but but—the Republicans. The Democrats. Yeah, yeah, okay, and please just stop that.

It's true, however, republicans are fuel on the fire of this march with their supply-side economics. But so, too, are the democrats, with their 'third way'. Or, am I wrong? Did the democrats not hold a majority in both houses for Obama's first two years? And the best they could manage, with only having their own party in opposition to righting what needed to be righted, was—Obamacare? Universal healthcare, with a democratic majority, couldn't even get a sniff of—maybe? Corporate reform? Such that we do not now have record levels of stock buybacks, unheard of CEO packages, when weighed against real wages that have remained stagnate since the late '70s. Record levels of income inequality, hand-in-hand with record levels of poverty—in May of 2016 (note the date), the IMF issued the USA a warning regarding its high levels of poverty, especially among the young. Massive tax breaks for corporations. Nope, nope, and nope. But we did get corporate bailouts, because—too big to fail. And here I thought, in America, socialism was a bad idea?

Accountability. Where is it? Because it matters. But no, what we get is—team politics: Young angry 'Berniebro' (someone please take the pen away from the person at the Atlantic that smeared these people) you had better vote for Hillary (if you love and care about America) or we'll get Donald Trump, and then, how will you sleep at night? And ... just how well did that work out?

I don't know, Boomer Person—when will you die? A little harsh? Perhaps, but also true. The divide is age. For when throughout this lovely experiment known as the human race has one generation not risen up, in ideals, against the older generation—their parents? And that's what we have now. That's the divide. One that's also fueled by ... Yes, I know I was able to pick the low-hanging fruit of cheap tuition in terms of real dollars and a job market in an economy that wasn't titled against me and although I know that's not the case for you, I'm really good in life right now and I'd like to stay that way, please. How else can you explain the continued support of those that have been in power the last forty years that have brought us to where we are now? Accountability. Show it to me. Where is it, because I just don't see it. Do you?

Here's the scorecard: Healthcare: 37th best in the world, while spending a higher portion of its GDP on this than any other nation. Children's survival, health, education, and nutrition: 39th best in the world. Wealth inequality: 71st. Life expectancy: 46th. Poverty: 13.4 percent, with only 25 other countries having substantially higher and more extreme rates of poverty. Human

Freedom Index: 17th. Freedom of the Press: 42nd. Accountability? Where? I'm waiting ...

There are three pillars of any just society, and each one must be held up and protected by the will of the people—always. Education, healthcare, and welfare. No matter what. Why? Because these are the things that help promote the greatest participation in a society by the most people, in the healthiest, most productive way. And that equals growth and opportunity for the most people, which then equals prosperity, for a nation. In other words, Main Street is the engine that drives an economy, not Wall Street.

And so, yes, there's only two parties, true—but not true. Democrats, listen to me carefully, republicans ARE NOT THE PROBLEM. And yes, we all know it has become the party of the whacked-out write-offs. It is, however, you, that is the problem. And here, I do not mean the Boomers—the Establishment Democrat voter, for as we have seen, they have no apparent interest in looking at results—accountability, and are interested only in their own status quo. No, it is the progressives whose hands I hold to the fire. Bernie blinked, and here we are today. And by this, I mean, it was his achilleas heel, the need to be accepted by the establishment. One that clearly wanted nothing to do with him—or you. Except, of course, to co-op your vote. To hold a gun to your head and say, vote for our candidate, or you will be responsible for electing that big bad man over there wearing a red tie. And again, how did that work out? And so, now it is time for you, youth of America, to wake up and demand accountability. You are the single largest cohort in American history—it is yours for the demanding. It's yours for the taking. Get your candidate through the democrat primaries, or, if the DNC obstacles are too great to allow this to happen—leave the party. One, or the other, for a divided Democratic Party is no longer of use to anyone. In fact, it's keeping America broken. You are the last ones standing, and it is your time now to make a difference. It is you, who can fix America, and stop this madness; this march toward fascism. And to you, my beautiful Boomer brothers and sisters, I leave you this: "A society grows great when old men plant trees whose shade, they know they shall never sit under." – Greek proverb.

“Nobody has ever measured, not even poets,
how much the heart can hold.”
— Zelda Fitzgerald

Thank you:
Nathalie Guilbeault and Alana Doyle.

Montreal Publishing Company publishes works of poetry, drama, fiction, and non-fiction. We seek writers that dare, and make us think—reconsider.

Relevance without fear.

Montreal Publishing Company

montrealpublishing.com

A Note From the Publisher:

Thank you for reading, *What I Know About the Human Race.* Should you wish to include it in your book club, get in touch, and let's see what we can help you with.

info@montrealpublishing.com

If you'd like to leave a review, that would be most appreciated, and you can do that here:

Goodreads
Amazon

If you'd like to keep up with what's going on with Christian Fennell, he can be found at:

christianfennell.com

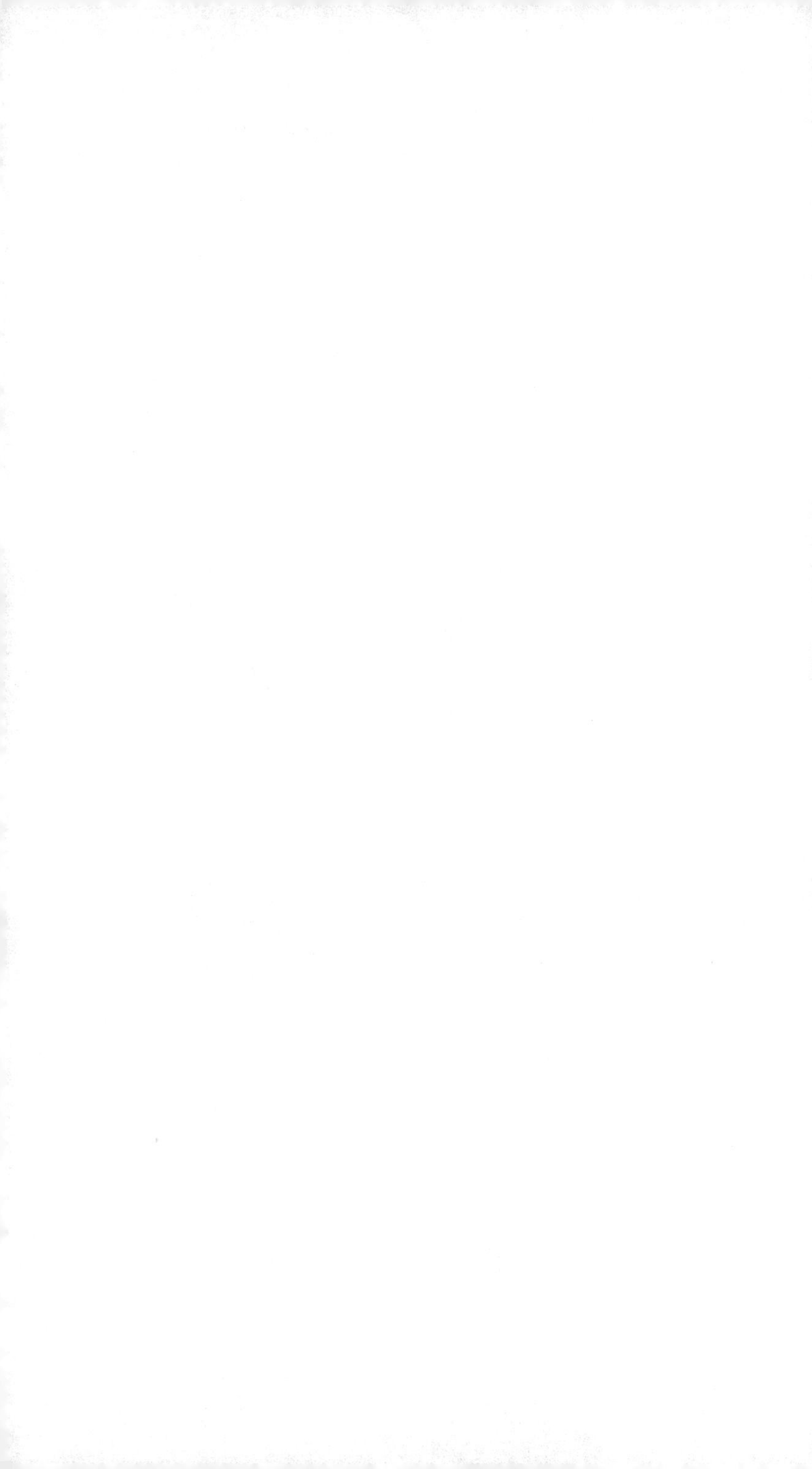

www.ingramcontent.com/pod-product-compliance
Lightning Source LLC
Chambersburg PA
CBHW030930060726
47591CB00005B/1735

* 9 7 8 1 9 9 8 3 5 3 0 0 2 *